Clay and Star

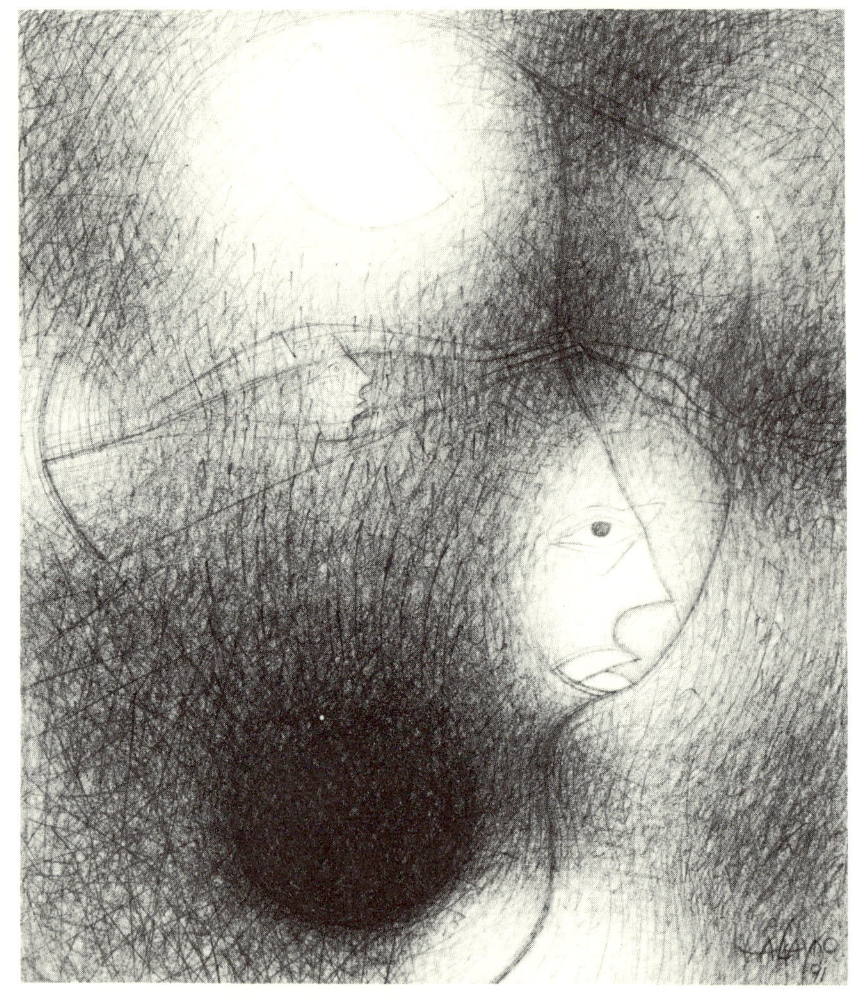

Clay and Star

CONTEMPORARY BULGARIAN POETS

Translated and Edited by

Lisa Sapinkopf and Georgi Belev

Introduction by Charles A. Moser

MILKWEED EDITIONS

Clay and Star

Printed in the United States of America.
Published in 1992 by Milkweed Editions.

Milkweed Editions
528 Hennepin Avenue, Suite 505
Minneapolis, Minnesota 55403
Books may be ordered from the above address.

ISBN 0-915943-85-9

95 94 93 92 4 3 2 1

We are grateful for the generous sponsorship of *Clay and Star* by the Witter Bynner Foundation and the Wheatland Foundation.

Publication of this and other Milkweed books is made possible by grant support from the Literature Program of the National Endowment for the Arts, the Cowles Media / Star Tribune Foundation, the Dayton Hudson Foundation for Dayton's and Target Stores, Ecolab Foundation, the First Bank System Foundation, the General Mills Foundation, the I. A. O'Shaughnessy Foundation, the Jerome Foundation, The McKnight Foundation, the Andrew W. Mellon Foundation, the Minnesota State Arts Board through an appropriation by the Minnesota Legislature, the Northwest Area Foundation, and by the support of generous individuals.

Library of Congress Cataloging-in-Publication Data

Clay and Star : contemporary Bulgarian poets / translated and edited by
Lisa Sapinkopf and Georgi Belev : introduction by Charles A. Moser.
p. cm.
Includes index.
ISBN 0-915943-85-9 (paper)
1. Bulgarian poetry—20th century—Translations into English.
I. Sapinkopf, Lisa. II. Belev, Georgi. III. Title: Clay and star.
PG1145.E3C57 1992
891.8'11308—dc20 92-4153
CIP

Acknowledgments

The translators wish to thank the many individuals and institutions whose multifaceted support made the realization of this book possible.

Alexis Levitin (SUNY Plattsburgh), Rosanna Warren (Boston University), and Daniel Weissbort (University of Iowa) painstakingly read and commented on the translations. It is difficult to express sufficient gratitude to them for their generosity, for the contribution their keen eyes and ears made to the book, and for their inspiration and encouragement over the years as teachers and friends.

Christopher Ricks (Boston University) read and made perceptive comments on the manuscript.

Thomas Butler (Cambridge, Massachusetts), Mark Elson and Grace Fielder (University of Virginia), and Martha Forsyth (Newton, Massachusetts) shared their expertise on Bulgarian linguistics, history, and culture.

The following extended gracious hospitality and/or invitations to give presentations of the work-in-progress: Gabriel Berns (University of California at Santa Cruz), Jo Berryman (California Institute of the Arts), Kathy Kelm (Nantucket Island School of Design and the Arts), Edward Czerwinski (SUNY Stonybrook), Roland Flint (Georgetown University), Frank MacShane (Columbia University), the National Women's Book Association, Jack Powers (Stone Soup Poets & Boston Mayor's Office of Arts and Humanities), James Ragan (University of Southern California), Rainer Schulte (University of Texas at Dallas), Richard Schupbach (Stanford University).

The translators warmly thank the University Professors Program of Boston University for supporting them with stipends while the book was in progress, and the American Translators Association for awarding the manuscript of *Clay and Star* first prize in their 1991 competition.

Special thanks to Vanya Vassileva for the photographs—and for her enormous help in gathering and forwarding books and manuscripts and overseeing numerous logistical details in Sofia. Thanks also to Marie Vassilev of Belmont, Massachusetts, for helping us get hold of otherwise unobtainable books.

Thanks to Jusautor, the Agency for Author's Rights in Sofia, Bulgaria, for securing permissions from the authors of the poems in this collection.

The translations in *Clay and Star* first appeared in the following journals: *Agni*, "Lake" and "Love" by Georgi Belev, "A Scene" by Ani Ilkov, and "Memory, Part II" by Marin Georgiev; *Black Warrior Review*, "Beneath Winter's Roof" by Ekaterina Iosifova and "Solitary Man" by Boris Hristov; *Carolina Quarterly*, "Clay and Star, Part 3" and "Villages Like Ghosts" by Ivan Davidkov; *Connecticut Poetry Review*, "At Night" by Boris Hristov; *Crab Creek Reviews*, "Garden of Questions" by Ivan Metodiev, "A Sign from Heaven" by Boris Hristov, "Morning" by Miriana Basheva, and "A Tale That's Not a Tale" by Binyo Ivanov; *Delos*, "The Tiny Man" by Ivan Radoev, "*And when the winter wind...*" by Georgi Borisov, "Safety Pins" by Radoi Ralin, "Height" by Nedelcho Ganev, and "The Wonderful in Poetry, or A Victim of Goldfish" by Konstantin Pavlov; *International Quarterly*, "Some Day" by Ivan Davidkov, "Ballad for Dialectical Materialism" and "Ballad for the Future" by Ivan Radoev, "The Warmth" by Petar Alipiev, "Misery" by Rumen Leonidov, "Teenagers" and "Ortamezar" by Ivan Teofilov, and "Interview from the Belly of a Whale" by Konstantin Pavlov; *Nimrod*, "The Old City" by Ivan Teofilov and "Monastery" by Ivan Davidkov; *Paintbrush: A Journal of Poetry, Translation and Letters*, "It Was War" by Miriana Basheva, "Gates" and "The Horse" by Georgi Borisov, "Who Cares for the Blind Stork" and "Interior with Faded Colors" by Blaga Dimitrova, "Vulnerability" by Fedya Filkova, "Silence" and "Riverbend" by Marin Georgiev, "Blue Pond at Berkovitsa" and "Beacon" by Vladimir Levchev, "Green and Gold" and "Evaporations" by Ani Ilkov, "If the Silence Should Suddenly Return" by Ekaterina Iosifova, "These Things from Words" and "This Crow" by Ivan Metodiev; *Partisan Review*, "The Wind Is Coming and I Love You" by Binyo Ivanov and "Four Seekers of the Great Metaphor" by Vladimir Levchev; *Poetry*, "Tale" and "Train" by Georgi Belev; *Vision International*, "*Three mares . . .* " by Danila Stoyanova and "Miracle" by Nikolai Kanchev.

Clay and Star

A Few Words on Poetry and Politics

In the Western world we do not normally think of lyric poetry and politics as closely linked. And to a considerable degree we are correct in overlooking that connection, for it is both subtle and contingent. But it does exist, and in rather more visible form in Bulgarian culture than in those of Western Europe and the United States. I should like to say a few words about it by way of an introduction to this excellent sampling of the work of a number of contemporary Bulgarian poets which you now have in your hands.

Over the last 150 years or so, Bulgaria has nurtured a strong poetic tradition (as it has, incidentally, more recently in the areas of vocal performance and the graphic arts). It is difficult for us Americans to comprehend the power of that tradition, since our own lyric poetry occupies a very small corner of our cultural consciousness. (It does emerge publicly once in a while, as when Robert Frost participated in the inauguration of President John F. Kennedy.) But the Bulgarian tradition is powerful enough to bring forth some extraordinary poets, even in a small country and under very difficult circumstances. This anthology itself bears witness to that fact, since it contains samples of the work of poets who have lived most or all of their lives under a political regime thoroughly hostile—not merely indifferent—to the poetic mind.

Perhaps I should elucidate a bit further what I see as the connection between politics and lyric poetry. The link lies in words. More precisely, it consists of the succinct and at the same time energizing use of words: individual words, brief phrases, occasionally a sentence, rarely as much as a short poem. A successful politician is a skillful handler of words for political purposes, one who can encapsulate political aims in a memorable phrase which lodges in the collective consciousness and influences people's thinking thereafter—phrases such as *manifest destiny, New Deal, New Frontier*. Such phrases both energize contemporaries and shape the ways in which we remember the periods when they were current. In similar fashion, a lyric poet rivets our attention with a memorable simile, phrase, or sentence, capturing universal human experience in language which the ordinary reader is incapable of formulating, but whose value he recognizes instantly. The successful lyric poet, like the successful politician, is one who can compact widespread experience into a few memorable words. We know the answer to Boris Hristov's question (see "The Window" in this volume): "Who helps us/see anything—here, in heaven, or in the infinity of art?"

If there is a vital connection between lyric poetry and politics, there is a tension between them as well. The political use of language is oriented toward the collective, whereas poetic language is rooted in an individual vision. It seems to me that it is here we must search for an explanation of the fact that political phrases tend quickly to be emptied of energy and originality, while the true poet's words stand the test of time. For the lyric poet is preeminently a person of private vision, one who upholds the primacy of the single poetic consciousness against the collective. Language is, after all, at once collective and individual. It must be collective if we are to understand one another, but it is style—especially linguistic style—which defines the individual person. The poet is the defender of individualism in language.

In American culture we tend to think of the poet as reclusive (Emily Dickinson) and a little odd (Robert Lowell). In the Slavic cultures, including Bulgarian culture, the poet is much more of a public figure and often becomes a political leader as well as a poet. A fine example is Hristo Botev—born on the remarkably appropriate date of December 25, 1848—who was simultaneously Bulgaria's finest nineteenth-century lyric poet and most dedicated revolutionary, a man who gave his life for the Bulgarian cause in 1876. Both his poetry and his life were an extraordinarily intense fusion of the political and the personal, so that he embodies the link of which I have spoken to the highest possible degree.

Had he lived past the Liberation, Botev would no doubt have been disappointed in his countrymen, much as was the national writer Ivan Vazov (1850-1921). Vazov was a great many things, among them a political figure and a lyric poet, but a poet who dedicated much of his poetry to the instilling of patriotic feeling in his countrymen. The lyric impulse at a high level also joined with political commitment in the life of Peyo Yavorov (1878-1914), one of Bulgaria's best natural poets who worked for the cause of Macedonian liberation.

After the October revolution of 1917 in Russia, several Bulgarian poets committed themselves to the proletarian cause early on. One of them was Hristo Smirnenski (1898-1923), a pure soul who dreamed of a society in which the downtrodden could live in dignity. Another was Nikola Vaptsarov (1909-1942), executed for communist partisan activity during the Second World War. Taking their cue from the outstanding Russian poet Vladimir Mayakovski, men like Smirnenski and Vaptsarov dedicated both their poetic gift and their lives to the cause of the dispossessed of this world, which they mistakenly believed would be truly advanced by the Communist movement. Put another way, they eliminated the tension between the poetic and the political within their work by resolving it in favor of the political.

For a poet with any conscience, the outcome of such a resolution was death, whether in the artistic or literal sense. Mayakovski took his own life in 1930. Smirnenski died very young of tuberculosis, and Vaptsarov died before a firing squad; both passed from the scene before 1944, which saw the beginnings of the introduction of a totalitarian system throughout the country.

After 1944, when lyric poets were compelled to eliminate the tension between the personal and the collective, they faced only two choices, either of which was destructive. One was to embrace the communist cause unreservedly. However, if one retained any sense of the good, such a step could lead to physical death. An example of this consequence is the brief career of Penyo Penev (1930-1959), who committed suicide when he could no longer conceal from himself how drastically socialist reality in Bulgaria diverged from his ideals. Another is Veselin Andreev (1918-1991), long known as the bard of the communist partisans of World War II, who took his own life when he finally recognized the range of disasters which the communist system he supported had visited upon his country.

The second choice after 1944 was to retreat into silence during the worst Stalinist years and then to concentrate upon the private at the expense of the collective. The great example here was set for Bulgarian poets by Atanas Dalchev (1906-1978). A man with an established poetic reputation before 1944, Dalchev refused to publish anything at all during the worst years of the repression—which was a form of artistic death. But once he began publishing again, on more private topics, he inspired a group of younger poets who came into prominence in the 1960s (some of them are represented in this collection) as they painstakingly sought to restore the foundations of the poetic tradition within Bulgarian culture. Lyubomir Levchev began as one of them, but later transformed himself into a literary functionary. However, he did have a son, Vladimir—also in this volume—who has done much to rebuild his family's poetic reputation. Another was Konstantin Pavlov, who became famous as an unwavering dissident, impervious to the blandishments of the political system. These men and others represented here restored the tradition for the next generation of poets from the 1970s and 1980s, who are well represented in this collection. They have advanced the process of working back from the retreat into the self, which is always a temptation for the lyric poet, and toward the life-giving tension between the individual and the collective which is so necessary both for poetry and for politics.

With the profound changes in Bulgarian cultural life over the last two years, it has become possible for lyric poets to help revitalize both Bulgarian culture and Bulgarian politics. Some have made direct political contributions: Radoi Ralin, for example, is a familiar figure on the political hustings, and Blaga Dimitrova was elected vice president of Bulgaria in 1992. But most will work indirectly: they are the ones who can rejuvenate the imaginations and the vocabularies of their countrymen, stunted and stereotyped by the totalitarian years. Of all writers, lyric poets pay the closest attention to the nuances of individual words and phrases, and that emphasis upon the individual is just what is much needed now in Bulgaria.

I write as a literary historian who looks for common threads in the development of Bulgarian lyric poetry. But the individual poet is ultimately a mystery perhaps best defined by negatives and by questions, as Stefan Tsanev shows us in a poem included in this volume:

> When a poet is born
> only mothers cry,
> they veil themselves with the dusk,
> stare in horror at the empty cradles—
> for themselves they've created nothing—
> when a poet is born.

In the final accounting the reader must read each individual poet as a separate voice and seek, through the medium of language, to share a unique vision of aspects of our common humanity.

Charles A. Moser
The George Washington University
Washington, DC
1992

Translators' Note

Bulgaria is a small country in southeastern Europe. Both its population—about nine million—and its size are roughly that of Ohio. Its capital, Sofia, has the same latitude as Boston. One of its five mountain ranges, the Rhodopes, was the legendary home of Orpheus. Located at the geographic, cultural, and political crossroads that are the Balkans, Bulgaria is bordered on the north by Romania, on the west by Serbia and Macedonia, on the east by the Black Sea, and on the south by Greece. Turkey, which shares a small part of Bulgaria's southern border, dominated Bulgaria for five hundred years. The country was liberated from the Turks in 1878 and reemerged as a European state with a constitutional monarchy. This was followed by a brief sixty-six years of independence before the Soviet army imposed, at the end of World War II, one of the most severe Communist regimes in Eastern Europe. Since 1989, Bulgaria has been moving to democracy along with the other Eastern European countries. It now has a multiparty democracy and a freely elected president (the philosopher Zhelyu Zhelev) and vice president (the poet Blaga Dimitrova).

▪

Bulgaria has a literary tradition of more than a thousand years. Old Bulgarian, sometimes called Old Church Slavonic, was the first written Slavic language and had a rich and thriving religious literature from the tenth through the fourteenth centuries until the invasion of the Turks. For the next several centuries, while Bulgaria was incorporated into the Ottoman Empire, the literary tradition was kept alive in monasteries. While still under the Turks, a national renaissance movement was under way in the eighteenth and nineteenth centuries, which saw the beginnings of modern Bulgarian literature. The modern literary language, in contrast to some Western European languages whose standards were imposed academically, is proudly and deeply rooted in the oral folk tradition (both spoken and sung), which survives to this day.

Bulgarian uses the cyrillic alphabet, which was invented in Bulgaria in the tenth century and later spread to Russia and throughout the Slavic world. Bulgarian grammar is remarkably different from that of the other Slavic languages. For example, it is the only Slavic language without a case system, and it is the only one to use definite articles. (These traits are shared by Macedonian, whose status as a distinct language or Bulgarian dialect is a subject of debate.) Interestingly, the absence of an infinitive verb form is a trait that Bulgarian shares with none of the other Slavic languages (except Macedonian) but that it does have in common with other languages of the Balkan region, such as Romanian, Greek, and Albanian, to which it is only distantly related linguistically through Indo-European.

▪

Our goal in compiling and translating *Clay and Star* was to celebrate the work of Bulgarian poets whose careers began or flourished during the years of stagnation under communism. The book focuses, although not rigidly, on those poets who managed, despite the ideological restrictions imposed on the arts, to keep their poetic integrity intact and to create an original, vibrant body of work. Rather than trying to present a superficial panorama of contemporary Bulgarian poetry, we were guided by the conviction that most readers' experience of the book would be richer and more meaningful if a smaller (although twenty-seven is hardly small!) number of poets were featured with more poems each, rather than the reverse. What we hoped to do was bring to the English-speaking world—for the first time, in the case of many of these poets—a personal selection drawn from this poetry of human and artistic triumph.

Alexander Gerov

Born in 1919. Alexander Gerov's was one of the most distinctive voices from the talented and prolific generation of the 1940s, and his career has continued unabated to this day. Characterized at times by an almost childlike simplicity, his poems are at once spontaneous and meditative, naïve and philosophical. Gerov has one of the widest followings of any living poet in Bulgaria.

Courtesy

You have lips like a drop of water.
And a white dove neck . . .
I step up, I doff my hat,
and start to drink the drop.

Accra

Let's go and live in Accra!
The African night attracts me.
I can see a spider, in our tiny hut,
deftly weaving a turban.

And in the reeds a flock of lanterns
is spreading pale golden rays.
The scorpions approach us
and watch us with peaceful eyes.

Mice

My old acquaintances the mice
are licking their lips in the attic.
They fray the threads of my thought,
they want to nip at my heart.

I'd love to discuss with them
what creator in the world thought us up,
that we should contradict each other's
life, instincts and thoughts?

But the mice keep silent. They don't speak.
They squeak, they're enjoying life.
Only cats with furious irises
seize them with flashing claws.

Birds

They don't plow, nor do they sow,
they only flap their wings,
but in spite of this they live,
and they don't live too badly.

Well, then? Either become a bird
or resign yourself at last
to sowing the best quality wheat
and to plowing your fields with a tractor.

Urban Tree

Is there a mind in you, universe?
There's no mind . . .
The starry night bends over me,
black, deep and huge.

And thousands of tangled birds
have gathered to sleep in the tree.
They huddle and in horror
cry their tiny souls.

A Problem

It's not so easy to die.
Death rules by its own law.
Once I got drunk. My heart
was pounding in my chest.

I thought it was going to burst.
But that wasn't death.
I was just waking up late,
my head as empty as a gun barrel.

Dandelion

Don't extend your thought
into time and space.
In them there's no sense, no happiness,
there isn't anything clear.

In the blooming dandelion
the cosmos is contained.
Be satisfied with this:
you understand its soul.

Eternity

Come lovely and soothing death.
—Walt Whitman

She's neither ugly nor fearful,
as they portray her the world over—
she is virginal and pure:
simple and calm is death.

You only have to soothe
all your thoughts into oblivion:
to lie down in clean bedclothes,
to close your eyelids, to fall asleep.

Maybe you won't reawaken,
won't pursue any new goal . . .
just dream for eternity,
the sun next to your heart.

Eye to Eye

What do you want from me?
Why, death, all these games?
I've already walked my path.
You know me through and through.

You can gather me up.
I'm ready for you.
It's enough for me
longingly to glimpse you.

It's enough for me,
bent over the exitless chasm—
my delight that this day
I'll vanish for good.

Matter

Death draws me to her.
Her great calm captivates me.
Wherever it touches,
rest and oblivion set in.

In a vast, sunny desert
I've already turned to ash.
Nothing hurts me anymore . . .
I was never born at all.

Blaga Dimitrova

Born in 1922. A poet, novelist, playwright, critic, and translator of Homer and of Polish and Swedish poetry, Blaga Dimitrova has published more than twenty books. Her work has been translated into most of the European languages, and a volume of her poetry was published in English by Wesleyan University Press in 1989. An outspoken opponent of the Vietnam War, Dimitrova was one of the most prominent dissident writers of the 1970s and 1980s. In 1992 she was elected vice president of Bulgaria.

8

The blind woman was closer to the sea
            than any of us.

They'd take her there,
leave her to be with it in private.
Her smiling face tilted
            toward its blue voice,
she'd sink in contemplation.

Its vague contour on the sand
was drowned by children's cries.
The infinite she measured with a nostril.
Her lips murmured with the waves
            as though in prayer.
The sea quivered on her lashes
            like a tear.

And the horizon with damp fingers
would read her face
            beyond its own line.

This and the following poem are from *Forbidden Sea*, a cycle of 59 poems.

18

Tossed out of the dream,
I woke up on this shore,
I met the glance of the sea
in a sprayed vineyard's hues.[1]

Beside me, like a warm
dune, a man's shoulder
surfaced—I leaned my cheek
against it to imprint my image
on its skin's soft sand.

Meanwhile another man sank
into my dream, one expelled
countless times with the subversive
complicity of time and distance.

The sea's steady pulse
swung me from shoulder to shoulder
as if between two sandy shores—
one present, manifest,
the other in the dream beyond.

And I, between the two of them—
above the chasm.

[1] Vineyards in Bulgaria used to be sprayed with a bright blue copper sulfate solution.

Interior with Faded Colors

"Why did you abandon me?"—
she reproaches the air
at the place where my father used to sit.

"If we were still young,
well, all right . . . but now, you see,
I can't live without you!"

And with her look fixed
on his voice, which never passed away,
she nods until she dozes off
                    on his breast.

Hotel Room

(Vienna, 1966)

They give you a number
as in a concentration camp.
You enter and become free—
the only possible freedom.

No imprint
of the previous guests.
No atmosphere—
but here, at last, you can breathe.

A sink, a bed, a wardrobe.
Ashen wallpaper.
Utter impersonality.
But here you gain your own face.

You switch on the bedside lamp.
You exchange words
with no one.
But you tremble in contact with the whole world.

No trace
will remain of you.
No memory.
But you'll remember your dream for years:

An endless kiss
next to the valises.
An unbreakable embrace,
your ticket in your pocket.

In the morning the sunlight
wakes you from an unfamiliar angle.
Where are you? A hotel room . . .
This is your true home.

Who Cares for the Blind Stork

Perched on the chimney on one leg,
as if impaled on a stake,
he doesn't see the weather vane beneath his nose,
takes no notice of the spiny antenna,
focuses his whole being, with his beak like a key,
toward the doorway to faraway spaces,
where a crowing pushes its way out of the dawn.
Don Quixote in plumed armor,
ready to flail his wings at windmills.
He has no inkling
of the clouds' conspiring huddles,
doesn't strain to hear the bickerings in the marsh,
and so, he always juts out from the bare chimney,
with no ill will toward the pungent smoke,
himself black as a chimney sweep.
Prized herald of happiness,
nothing troubles him—
if only he manages to pick up the sunrise
in his beak and deliver it everywhere—
a rosy-cheeked infant day
(in keeping with the belief).
There's just one thing I don't get—croaked a frog—
the mighty wind's razor,
the slanting rain's scythe . . .
why haven't they yet shorn his wings?

Sunstroke

In the heat ruddy circles
chiming cymbal-like
start spinning before my eyes
and suddenly while walking
it seems to me I'm drawing
with a compass on the planet
circle after charmed circle:
a horizon,
a hug,
a noose,
smoke.

Units of Measurement

From wing to outstretched
wing—
a bird's measure
of the horizon.

From palm to nailed
palm—
man's measure
of the universe.

Grass

I'm not at all afraid
of being stepped on.

Trodden grass
becomes a path.

Radoi Ralin

Born in 1923. A prolific writer of poetry, fiction, screenplays, and essays, Radoi Ralin had many of his works suppressed during the totalitarian era because of their satirical social content. He has been one of the leading intellectual figures during Bulgaria's political changes, working toward the restoration of democracy. Rare for a contemporary poet, his popularity is such that he is recognized in the streets. He has actively promoted the most promising young talents in various fields.

The Man Who Didn't Sign

In this old neighborhood
where poverty makes everyone brothers
and the child not yet walking
knows his fate,
where everyone knows how many sins
and shirts everyone owns—
where everyone awaits the Good Future
and tall and short alike signed against the war! For peace!

Only one man didn't sign.
How was this possible? A disgrace to the whole neighborhood!
With wounded hearts we set out,
we located him. We rammed his door open.

An invalid from the war,
he had no hands.

Home-Study Course in Freedom

Those who crawl are the freest!
They can crawl at will
wherever they want,
whenever they want,
for as long as they want.

Beneath them is the hard
earth.
The hard and fast earth.
The geologically examined
and historically proven
earth.
And they tickle her
agreeably
with their crawling.

Those who crawl are the freest.
Headwinds
don't affect their direction.
The sun doesn't blind them.
And most important,
they're not at risk
of falling . . .

They claim, with good reason,
their ideologue
to be Antaeus—
and he's a tough act to follow . . .

They're not vulnerable to falling,
like airplanes whose flights
are guided from below.

And the ants are so logical
in their freedom
they don't need to fly at all.
It never occurs to them
to even think about
earthquakes.

Ideological Tango

Side by side we stood together
beside the brand-new, well-greased lathe,
just the two of us . . .
you'd already begun to peel
our country's steel,
you taught me your technique
and promised yourself to me.

(Refrain): Those days were blessed
with beautiful dreams,
but you married another
and betrayed me.

The forest outside turns yellow with grief,
but in surpassing my quota I'll drown
my sorrow.
Nonetheless, for my country's steel's sake,
your technique will remain with me.
. . . And tomorrow, when you're divorced,
you'll cry for me.

Note: This parody of socialist-realist verse was written in 1954, the year of Stalin's death. (Stalin means "steel" in Russian.)

Safety Pins (excerpts)

1. Qualifications

Vladimirov was appointed
consul to Aden.
That such a place existed
he learned only then.

2. Expected Result

The poet unmasked the scoundrel
with a pointed epigram.
A hundred and two got angry;
the prototype kept mum.

3. Service Rewarded

The diligent translator
made his contribution.
Tolstoy got a B for style—
that was the retribution.

4. Children's Poet's Child

Poor, dear child
born to suffer on earth—
has to read everything
Dad brings forth.

5. A Concern

They're not impertinent or cosmic,
yet I'm troubled by these questions:
How do they eat, breathe, and multiply—
people without connections?

Seduced and Abandoned

I first fell in love with Dena, and hey—
she became an inspector's fiancée.
Then I went out with Tamara, and look—
as her husband she took a railroad cook.
With Vera I had a glorious time—
she made an engineer sign on the dotted line.

Temenuga I almost wed for life—
today she's a doctor's wife.
Dorotea would never look at a stranger—
she's living with a forest ranger.
Fanny and I were quite content—
now a professor pays her rent.

I cultivated Nadka so well,
that in with diplomats she fell.
Bistra and I made a wonderful pair—
now she gives joy to the chargé d'affaires.
Todora and I had a child on the way,
but she ran off with a machinist one day.

I'm a good luck charm, I hand out visas!
After me their life-style eases.
Only I'm single—though it's not what I want,
on my own behalf I'm a dilettante.
I make the rogues jealous when they see
how all the women flock to me.

Oh, if I myself had achieved some fame
I'd have an even higher aim.
But seduced and abandoned as I've been,
nothing but a trampoline,
I never managed to reach the top—
why couldn't one of them lift *me* up?

Ivan Davidkov

Born in 1926. Ivan Davidkov wrote twelve volumes of poetry, a series of novels, and essays, and he is renowned as a translator of Ukrainian, Belarusian, and Russian literature. His work has been translated in all the Eastern European countries, France, and the United States. Davidkov was also a talented painter; the visual detail and atmosphere of his paintings enrich his poetic works. He was known for his generosity and his support of the younger, experimental poets of recent decades. He died in 1990.

Returning from the Fair

Behind us the poplars lingered, the horses' neighs,
the noise from faded tents, the fakirs' shouts,
the swishing of the giant swings, the girls' swaying skirts,
and the young soldiers' glances darting after them.

Carts were overtaking us. Someone had bought
a goat, someone else was hauling bleating rams.
And gypsy men, their long legs splayed over the cart-rails,
played gleaming cornets.

Women from other villages were overtaking us, and men
with jackets draped over their arms
were leading them on shortcuts across the fields—
Why wear ourselves out on this dusty road?
—and the corn's yellowed leaves
shielded them from curious glances.

And the evening swelled with secret words
and rustlings of skirts pulled away
under someone's hand to reveal
the gleam of a thigh—and sounds of breathing
lingered in the flattened grass.

And stealthily I looked that way
and thought the moon about to rise
and that's why there was a shining in the stalks.

But it was slow. I don't know why.

3

I felt awakening in me at night
a tree tall as the sky;
constellations of golden ants
were crawling on its topmost branches,
and the roots, dense blue veins—
pierced my sleepless flesh,
tried to nail me to my cot,
to the road and to the stone,
but with lips clenched I pulled my legs free.
Were the roots of this tree rivers
for the sky-noise and gleam they carried,
and for the shoals of secrets lying beneath them?
Were they rivers, or were rivers those that led my soul
towards rocky islands of empty altars
where a single sea-pine ringing with the wind
floated up to take me in its dark boat?

I know my branches will give birth
not to a golden apple but to a startled
sigh of the wind. This fruit is perhaps the truest
because in it is the silence of the universe—
that bridge above time's chasm on which will pass
both the newborn's toddling cry
and the dry tear of the one traveling
towards oblivion . . .

I felt awakening in me
a tree tall as the sky.
It doesn't know her yet,
but fall will come to spill
its leaves—my slow-circling dreams—
and it will remain in the sky as white
as the skeleton of a giant fish
eaten bare by the stars' bristling ants.

This poem is from *Clay and Star*, a cycle of poems.

Monastery

All night long the drinking fountains gurgled,
All night long I tried to sleep—
the cypress kept piercing my dream.
As day broke I closed my eyes and barely heard
the staircase of the upper floor creaking—
the saints were coming down from the icons to go to bed.
Slowly they took off
their baggy, worn-out robes,
took off their halos so they wouldn't disturb their sleep
and hung them on the wall on nails
like children's hoops.

I slept just an hour, then awoke.
The light was banging on the window,
spilling across the ceiling.
From the shadow over my bed I could tell
that the old monk, the beekeeper, was returning.
He tottered, carrying honeycombs the color of juniper root.
It was such a fertile summer
that honey dripped onto the cobblestones
the way milk drips at dusk from the engorged udders
of the goats heading home.

And the fountains rocked the dawn in their basins.

Villages Like Ghosts

Villages like ghosts will chase each other through the foggy fields.
Leaves and birds' voices will cover the wet road.
And in your late dreams the horse won't rise,
the sun won't be grazing on the bare hills.

The foxes will squeeze through the roosters' crows.
The well will shine crowned with frost
and the naked cherry tree will ring in the sky like a lyre.
The fire will be like an apiary next to which
you'll gather your buzzing thoughts.
And when you set off in the morning, sensing the trembling
of the damp and bitter fallen leaves, you'll see
apples lying outside the door: that is your garden
harvested by the night.

Above the steep gully you'll see, plowing
his thorny plot, a peasant who has harnessed the shrieks
of jay and crow.

I

Where was it left—the key for us to open
the door of this vast summer
which I see beneath the rain and dusk
like an old and vacant house
with rust on the lock, dust on the steps.

For us slowly to climb up to the heat
of the nights, to the words
which brushed like fish past
our bodies, our tenderness,
our lips which remained breathless.
The pomegranate tree was ripening then in the yard,
and the room was filled with thinning dusk,
which made you elusive
as the driftings of night sand.

And I touched your body
as a peasant touches the hills in springtime,
his palm sensing how
the vineyards are standing up to comb
their green hair
with rain and wind—
and in their motion he feels the pagan cry
of the grape harvest
and the swirling red dance.

And at midnight the fishermen returned
from the wharf, they set at the doorsill
huge baskets which leaked
the shudderings of chasms and fish.
And the pomegranate slowly set off for the sky—
because it was late and the moon
hadn't yet risen above the world.

This poem is from *Tune for a Flute*, a cycle of poems.

Some Day

The wind will call me—and some day I'll depart
without saying good-bye. Acrid smoke
from unheard-of railway stations will be my fellow traveler,
and the mad galloping of cities past the train window.
And no one will be waiting for me in the evening cities,
but the sea gulls will fly before me to show me the way,
and stairways of port hotels
with friendly voices husky from the damp will talk to me.
There will be a café on the bay filled with sailboats,
and there will be a chair for me and a smile
in a mirror facing them.
By the railing tulips will flash their night-lights
so the wind, which had leafed through the cypress trees,
can reread their green dreams.
I'll smell seaweed in the words of people
whose shadows seek each other in the dark,
and my unfinished coffee will glance up at me
with the eye of a southern fish.

Meteor

Before you cry out, Stop—you'll fall on your back
and above your eyes the horse
with vast haunches will shine like a forest
set aflame by the falling leaves. You'll see
its bridle—two ropes stretched taut
between sky and earth on which
you'll be able to crawl tight-lipped
above the pain. You'll yank yourself like a nail
from the dry earth into which your last hour
hammers you. But your hands will touch
only the stallion's tired snorts,
the wind. You'll fall downwards
into yourself, and pierce this chasm
like a huge black meteor.

Your soul will leave on tiptoe
so as not to wake the outstretched body—
and your last cry will flash like a knife
jabbed into the sky's ribs.

Ivan Radoev

Born in 1927. One of the most highly regarded Bulgarian poets of the early 1950s, Ivan Radoev took a long hiatus from poetry after he was severely attacked by Marxist critics for publishing a cycle of love poems (instead of writing Socialist-realist verse in praise of leaders, factories, etc.). During this time he became a playwright with success in Bulgaria and abroad. Now with active careers in both genres, his poetry has shifted dramatically in style from his earlier lyrical poems in classic form to often ironic free verse.

Ballad for Dialectical Materialism

The time will come, after insomnias and strayings,
after long marches through mountains and epochs,
for the squadron to dismount.
The distance from stirrup to earth
will be strange to us.

We'll still be reeling from the head-on blows,
from the sad treacheries of sons and fathers,
from the free air
we swallowed with our tears for the dead—
we'll be dizzy.

Who are you?—history will ask us—
from which dynasty? Where are your medals?
Your architecture? Music? Painting?

We'll just smile through the pane of the air
sweat-filmed from the horses' puffing nostrils.

Then nature will paint us with our hands elongated,
with gladiators—Thracian, Mayan, Incan—
running in our eyes,
and above our heads she'll put a halo of mothers
whom we killed, out of pity, before we ourselves were killed.

Many words will become senseless (as they are already, by the way).
The future's language will be one of mathematical rigor.
Beneath the tiny electronic stars

will stand one brief equation:
the distance from earth to stirrup
equals the square of the distance from earth to sun.

"Mount up!"
A young boy will command—white, black or yellow.
And all the kids will straddle their wild sticks.

Ballad for the Future

Future—with what hands shall we pass you on?
You're very far, you can't make out our hands.
Our palms are clammy bank notes.
The lines of life, honor, duty and art
cross those of shame.
Under our nails is the mud from clawing
our way up to the point of our fall.
No one else but we ourselves
handcuffed us, comfortably, in the face of our fear.
That's why we offer you our two bound palms
instead of unfolded wings.

The only remnant
of shame we felt
was when we buried our mothers with communal fees.
Then we dared not put
our hands on their foreheads
so they wouldn't carry to the grave
the imprint of our horror.

Of course, there were shining ones among us.
They set off long ago, Future, to meet you.
But the ballad tells us
they went blind on the road . . .

Parable of the Poet's Reward

Before my eyes would often pass
the images of five women,
five sisters of my father—
five of my aunts.
Each one kneaded bread for at least twenty people.
They'd sweep the garden.
Their legs had
blue, swollen veins.
The five of them are dead now.

Later on I saw the sea,
but the blue veins lingered in front of my eyes—
a blue like I'd never seen.
I thought:
just one more drop
and they'll turn red.

They'd sweep the garden clean
of ghosts and lizards
and on the whitewashed wall they'd leave
their veins
which slithered onto the trellis,
and the sun would jump into the grapes.

Then they'd empty apronfuls of apples onto the porch.
Apples so red they could scarcely keep from turning blue.
Blue, red; blue, red . . .
Through the cleaned yard three rivers would start flowing—
a blue, a red . . . and a golden one.

The red one gave birth to foals,
the blue one, piglets,
the golden one . . . I had no idea—
and I'd wait, lost in reverie,
until my grandmother would light the oil candle
and give me a slap to break my insomnia.

The Sweater

The sick man's lamp guides death.
Ten years! The woman is knitting a sweater.
An angel. With ball and chain.
Stitch by stitch she prays.

She has the strength for one more breath, but he,
smiling from the North Pole, keeps watching her hands.
The dying man's will is cruel.

The woman drops her stitches into non-Euclidean space.
The world unravels in a thousand hypotheses.

For whom do the angels knit?

The Tiny Man

A tiny man!
He arranges your dream and your day.
With tiny eyes he opens the world.
He introduces you. Gives you permissions.
Buys and pays,
takes off your skin with cold fingers,
sleeps between himself and your wife,
gets you up, shaves his beard on your face,
drinks his tea from your cup,
puts on your shoes in the morning—
and you set off with tiny footsteps
to take your wings
to the cobbler's.

A tiny man!
A very tiny man!
Grinning, sweating, slimy, loathsome.
You could step on him whenever you like.
But you're careful.
Because he's
yours.

Petar Alipiev

Born in 1930. Petar Alipiev's early lyricism remained unswayed by the experimental trends of some of his contemporaries in the "April Generation" (so-called because it flourished after the Party Plenum, held in Sofia in April 1956, when the Communists condemned the "cult of personality" of Stalin and his Bulgarian counterparts). Uniquely unprolific, he has published just one volume, *Lirika*, which has been reissued several times with new poems added.

Old Man

On his tired memory a splendid
vision floats: well-muscled, hairy,
huge-chested he lifts, before his astounded
fellow-villagers, a cart with its rails
removed. The wheels spin high
off the ground, the shaft shudders
and warps. The children swallow, rapt,
as he circles them triumphantly.

Then, unsummoned, trenches,
fairs, caskets, weddings, women
once-loved return. And all of this struggles
to dislodge the prior vision.
But he gathers his last strength to beat back
the things lived in other years,
and with cart held high
he strides down the corridors of eternal fog.

The Warmth

In the orchard,
raked and trenched,
the dry burning branches
squeezed smoke into the sky.

Sluggish, from the earth emerged
a lizard rusty as the leaves.
He stood stunned close to the warmth
that had broken his winter sleep.

Glancing at the sparking flame
so wished for, so unexpected,
he sensed life, and dashed
in pursuit of living.

With eyes agape
he turned mindless toward the fire;
solemnly he entered it,
and became darkness and light.

Ivan Teofilov

Born in 1931. The ancient city of Plovdiv, where Ivan Teofilov was born, figures prominently in his poetry. Trained as an actor, he was a famous playwright in the 1960s until one of his plays created such a political scandal that both his poetry and his plays were unofficially banned. He then became director of an internationally acclaimed puppet theater. He has published seven volumes of poetry and is a renowned translator of turn-of-the-century Russian poetry into Bulgarian.

The Hills

Unrepeatable, ever-present mirage
in the glorious Thracian harvests.
Obscure utterance of Creation—
which in the beginning was the Word.
Deep tombs of men and buildings,
gleaming steps of human love and buildings. And hills!
Three arcs, one handful, a whole world.
Flavia, Ulpia, Tremontium—names!
Ploden. Neokoria. Filipopol—names!
Hills—three arcs, one handful, a whole world.
Book of knowledge, clover of storms.
Key. Foundation. Repository. Fragment of life
linked to other life. Until now, and from now on—
circles of life, unrepeatable, constant.
Life of stone, of wind, of rose, of grapevine,
of an emperor's ring, of spurs,
of horses' bones, of marble sayings,
Roman numerals, Turkish fountains, mosaic floors,
of oat-seed, stone and wind . . .

This and the following two poems are about Plovdiv, which was built on three hills in southern Bulgaria and is one of the most ancient Balkan cities.

The Old City

Your ancient tiers climb among the stars,
small blue donkeys graze the silence,
a Roman street twists down among the wedding candles,
a cry of woman's flesh issues from the clock,
purple landowners recline in their deep houses,
they can hear the pig, the hen, the train, the mouse.
The darkness is rising, its pupils sensual and quick,
the wedding veil flies on the chimneys' breath,
the blue donkeys scamper on moonlit roofs.
Saints with bleeding lambs soar up
from white churches to meet the wedding veils,
leopards with eyes of amber watch from the gates.
Bacchantes with satin headbands pour
fragrant myrrh from bronze jars among the boxwoods . . .

Ortamezar—The Jewish Quarter

Neighborhood
of tiny shaded yards
beside sweltering watermelon plots,
circles of wells like carousel horses,
drowsy, littered streets—
and the charmed,
despotic
church.
Neighborhood
of Turkish ways and synagogue,
promised land of shopfronts full
of chickpeas,
caramels,
rock candy.
Neighborhood
of fear and anguish
where stars shone in the daylight
(as in the time of the saints)
on the poor Jews' coats,
of exterminations of crows,
of air raid sirens, shelters,
of the huge eyes of my childhood . . .
They shot Sammy, son of Yakov,
brother of Esther and Bekka
(the twin redheads) on our rooftop.
We later learned
he'd changed his name to Angel—

and this bleeding, silenced angel landed on our house. My grandmother crossed herself and I saw the spared crows fly overhead. A magnificent sunset blazed. Damn!—my father muttered.

In Yakov's window
seven colored candles burned.
It was Passover.

Turkish Bath in Ortamezar

Subterranean catacombs
bursting with milky steam.
The neighborhood Adam is returning to the Creation,
his unfamiliar image
transported on deafening wooden sandals.
Bodies in zealously hygienic poses
behind matte sheets of mist.
Twin spigots gush into marble basins
that overflow in careless floods,
dropped copper wash-bowls
resound like gunshots,
there's chatter all around you
but you can't make out the words
up close, your gaze seeks them
in the dome where the colored glass
throbs in the radiant rose-window.
But a sudden burst of steam
makes the words sink, the glass
shimmer with faded longings
and seeing echoes in the milky darkness.
A moment later, when the fog
clears through special vents,
the magic circle is restored
on the misted dome.
And brimming with words of thanks
you peer into the old *hamam*[1]—into life
lit up by singing tubs and simple gestures,
by ancient human silence.

[1]The Turkish name for public bath.

Teenagers

On our way home from the factory,
we'd always stop at that bridge and wait
for the train to pass. It would pull into view,
the metalwork would shudder, and clinging
to the sharp crosspoints of the railing,
we'd scream at the top of our lungs,
and, just to show the passengers how easy it was,
we'd jump into the river,
and then roll over and over in the sand
while the world grew mute
and the memory of the train sank into nothingness.
We'd unwind completely, we could feel
our exhaustion, and that of all space,
crumble in the crunching sand.
Frogs would sing their solos
from the magic corners of the stillness,
then at last we'd see the sunset
spread incredibly fast above us
like the branches of a vast sea-pine,
and we'd be drawn deep into its redness.
We'd slowly rise to our feet, pull
our sailor shirts up over our heads
like kids, slip off our greasy pants,
and stride like men toward the gleaming,
hushed, caressing water.

Shared Existence

Cold crests with deep-cut corridors
and then the rejoicing, as though dreamt,
of the rounded peaks. The shift in sound—
from water to cricket. Grass—a sun in bloom.
A descent towards the unknown—
the same exclaiming earth.
Hamlets set in harsh geography,
clambering, crooked, with the thinned
divinity of rock silhouettes
echoing the mules and cocks, ragged
from landslides and stones.
A sky mulls itself over, incense smoke shields the distance
that slips into its landscape.
Human forms quiver in the heat,
the asphalt reeks, a steamroller shudders.
And the hay-gatherers, seated
in the meadow's gleam, ate their lunch
with familiar gestures, their parched
eyes shaded by coarse kerchiefs.
Joyful shared existence—life that surges
from stone and water, from ancient memory,
from unclouded mind, from trees and grass . . .

untitled

The falcon! His symmetrical confession—
circles of light and vertigo . . .

The wind's wedding band.

Hoarse hymn
of air and rock.

Up there!

But down here,
in their brief spans within spacious life
hardly anyone will know the breath
of ant or clover—
equally confessions—
and lit-up thought and quickening pain
and heated circles of love . . .

beneath the avalanche of sun and the echoes
of the vastness—which seem
another memory of theirs! And soul!

Konstantin Pavlov

Born in 1933. Konstantin Pavlov was one of the most famous poets of the 1960s. His two early books of satirical visions of the Communist order attracted such a devoted underground following that his publications were banned for years. During this time he turned to screenplay writing (experimental art films in particular) and won several international screenwriting awards. He has recently been able to resume publishing his poetry due to the political changes in Bulgaria, and his latest book, in 1991, was published in an unheard-of ten thousand copies.

√ The Wonderful in Poetry, or A Victim of Goldfish

No one publishes my poems,
no one reads them.
They're dangerous.
They arouse base instincts
and corrupt the soul
(in the words of one
who'll appear in due course).
They're especially harmful to children.
And adults.
My friends have abandoned me.
The girls have stopped loving me.
A widow even called me the demonic type.

So as not to be lonely,
I bought three goldfish.
In a glass bowl.
I fed them waterbugs
and changed their water.

Once
my landlady's scruffy cat
snuck in and nabbed
the prettiest, the most playful.
The remaining two would dash in horror
when they heard the insidious beast.
But I guarded them with the greatest care.

One rainy evening,
out of melancholy,
out of I don't know what,
I decided to read out loud
a poem I'd written that day.

Mocking myself,
I bowed down before them
and asked:
would you permit me to recite a poem?
I read them a cynical,
anti-societal poem
(in the words of one
who'll appear in due course).
When I looked up at them
my face froze in shock—
they had turned grayish black,
grown huge jaws
and sharp teeth,
they looked like baby sharks.
They wouldn't touch the waterbugs
I poured out for them,
they spurned my bread crumbs.

So I seized the landlady's scruffy cat
and hurled it at them.
The poor creature was torn to shreds
in seconds.
From that day on, this was
their favorite food.

Each evening I'd read them
my depraved poems
(in the words of one
who'll appear in due course).
They grew bigger and bigger,
beastlier and beastlier;
they became real sharks.
The aquarium could scarcely contain them,
and cats no longer satisfied them.
From then on

everything fell into place.
I read them my most dangerous poem of all,
and the glass began to crack, then it shattered.
The sharks leapt out,
the gentler of the pair spread its jaws
and gulped me down
while the other devoured the wardrobe
where an informer was huddling.

Adaptation

Quick!
We're due at the square,
The square with mighty fountains,
Mighty fountains gushing odors
Of roses and benzaldehyde.
We've got to be there at 5:30.
Sharp. Just as the invitation said—
5:30!
(They painted the circles last night—
I saw them.)
The walking will begin at 5:30 sharp.
The invitation said so—
5:30 sharp.
Soft music will melt our bones,
A soft voice will gently urge:
"Relax . . .
Relax completely . . ."
We'll each walk around in our own circle,
We'll beat ourselves with gentle blows.
And wracked with guilt, nearly suicidal,
We'll recount our past crimes.
And in the middle of the square,
Right smack in the middle,
Virgins in white tunics
Will dance, my dear, will dance—
Symbols of purification!
Later it will turn out for sure
(For sure it will turn out later)
That these were actually men
In drag—
Not virgins.
But is their sex really important?—
It's the symbol,

The symbol that counts, my dear!
And
Deeply moved, we'll recount our past crimes;
We'll confess with vast relief
Our most heinous thoughts.
No one will listen to anyone else—
We'll be talking to ourselves.
And we'll be relaxed.
Completely relaxed.
The circular processions will continue
Till the moment,
The very moment, when we're all convinced
That words are no longer necessary—
And we won't think twice,
And thoughts won't torture us.
That two or three desires are sufficient.
Then I'll be satisfied
If you tell me boobooboo . . .
And you'll be satisfied
If I tell you poopoopoo . . .
And a single cow's contented moo
Will best express
That which has been troubling us
For twenty-odd centuries.
And now—
Let's lie down on the square
Let's drift collectively off to sleep
For two, three, five, six centuries.
There's no longer any need to dream—
Someone else will dream for us.
Our own nightmares!
He'll even interpret them for the world.
Incorrectly.

The End of Mythology

Lads and maidens rinsed their wounds
in the forest spring,
the nymphs recoiled from the blood
before the first cock crowed,
they dashed off naked and sought refuge,
enchanted and fair,
in the arms of the police.

Lads and maidens faced the bullets
with hoarse song,
and the hero who nursed
for fifteen, twenty, thirty
(I forget how many) years,
died on his devoted mother's
shriveled breast.

Interview from the Belly of a Whale

"Where have you been,"
they ask me,
"for more than three decades?"

"I've been in the belly of the Whale.
You can see that just fine,
you're asking out of spite."

"How," they ask me,
"have you spent
these three decades in his paunch?"

"This you know too.
I gambled,
with that gambler, Jonah, from the Bible."

"But Jonah got out!"
they exclaim.
"Why haven't we seen you around?"
they ask.

"Jonah got out.
God ransomed him,
and the devil didn't pay a chipped dime."

"Has it been scary,"
they ask,
"for so many decades?"

"It was scary,
it got boring.
I smoked and kept silent,
I kept silent and smoked."

"And what will you do now,"
they ask,
"for the next thirty years?"

"Me?
I have no idea.
But I do know that the Whale
will be spitting butts
for three decades
and fouling the marine
environment."

Lyubomir Levchev

Born in 1935. Lyubomir Levchev is the author of more than twenty books of poetry. Along with Konstantin Pavlov and Stefan Tsanev, he is part of the April Generation. He has been translated into many languages and given many awards abroad. For years he was president of the Bulgarian Writers Union.

Rooftops

—to B. Rainov

My grandfather's old house
had a roof of slate shingles.
And I even remember some weeds growing
up there . . .

—Where,
            I ask,
                        is my grandfather's old house?
And they reply that it fell to ruins
by itself.
            —See,
                        they say,
what an interesting walkway
we made out of the shingles!

. . . Of course, the shingles are the same.
But that the house caved in
by itself . . .
            I can't believe it!

It was a wonderfully conceived house—
homey,
simple,
human . . .
Yet, like my grandfather's universe
it too
        suffered from one flaw—
an awfully heavy roof,
but no foundation!

So the house didn't collapse,
it sank slowly,

slowly into the earth.
It sank up to its roof.
And today I walk like a cat on its shingles.
Boxwoods rise from the chimneys like smoke.
And down below,
                    in my grandfather's Atlantis,
everything is the same as back then.
The hearth is burning.
Beans are simmering in the pot.
And Dad,
            little,
                    is curled up in my grandmother's lap.
—Fall asleep quick!
                    she whispers,
because the vampire's walking on our roof! . . .
And Dad pricks up his ears in horror.
Yes—he hears it!
They're my footsteps.
And he believes her.
And shudders.
And falls asleep . . .

And I'm still rattling the paving stones.

It's awfully hard to design a roof
in such a way that it can support
the foundations of time.
The superstructure
                    (as Marx would say)
mustn't crush the base.
And we—who write—
we must create something very true,
realistic,

sunny,
and resilient . . .

Because it seems to me
                                        that
someone is already walking on our roof.
And lightning bolts,
like wings,
are sprouting from his shoulders.

Weasel

Just after me
and just before the big snow
she came to live in the same house
on the riverbank.

She arrived—
and the brazen flocks of rats
disappeared at once.
Thus we remained, only
she
and I.
She
and I . . .
In the house set apart,
with bullet holes in its balcony.

In the morning when,
shivering from the cold,
I'd go down into the deep cellar
to fetch firewood,
she'd hear me.
She'd emerge from the spigot
of the moldy wine cask.
Graceful
and red,
she'd gush like the ghost
of the wine long since drunk.

She'd approach
to an ax-length away
and . . .
I think she'd nod to me.

I'd greet her thus:

"Hello,
magical, rusty hermit . . . "

And . . .
I think she'd nod
and then dart away
because, as the old man said,
words kill the creative spirit.

Dénouement

You're undressing as though for the doctor.

The thought shatters in my soul.
And suddenly
everything becomes fragile.
The little vase becomes a test tube.
The flower, a strange bacterium.
And you burst out laughing:
"Come on now,
ask me how I feel.
What's ailing me.
Where I hurt . . .
Ask anything you like!
Just don't pretend . . . "

I bend down mechanically.
"Breathe,"
                I say.

The air draws you deeply into itself.
And you vanish.
The bed retains your warmth—
torn garment of the fugitive.
But you've wrenched yourself out.
For good.
Perhaps you're already sliding down
your memory.

You're crying.
The zipper of your skirt is broken.

And your voice is shattered.
I hear:

"Farewell, my love!
You I once longed for, farewell!
I wish you all the best—
and part of my pain."

Stefan Tsanev

Born in 1936. An innovative poet whose career began in the 1960s, Stefan Tsanev created provocative, often jarring works that reintroduced, in a vigorous new mode, some elements of the Bulgarian expressionist poetry of the 1920s, as well as of the Russian poet Mayakovski (whom Tsanev has translated into Bulgarian). He is also a playwright who has had several plays successfully staged in Eastern Europe.

Penguins

On the fake snowbank
the Sunday visitors
assemble
to watch the penguins,
and the penguins,
to watch the visitors.

Suddenly
a housewife has a realization:
"The penguins—they're like us!"

The penguins nod sympathetically:
"Yes—we were once
birds . . . "

Rehearsal for a Parade

One! two! three! . . . testing! One! two! three! . . . testing! One!

Into the empty square
on an armored personnel carrier
swoops
Lenin!

The commander of enthusiasm
addresses him sternly:
"Wave more energetically!
Focus your eyes more!
Your mouth! Don't forget to open your mouth! Like this . . .
Turn on the tape recorder!"

Náchali!

(Tovarishch Lenin, tak li vy nachali
v 17-om godu?)[1]

And from everywhere,
from all sides,
from all streets

throngs
a costumed Red Army,
costumed partisans,
and ordinary citizens, but looking costumed . . .
and they all rush toward the center of the square,

[1] Russian for: "Let's get started! (Comrade Lenin, is this how you started in 1917?)"

and they all shake their fists
in front of the mausoleum's empty rostrum . . .

(Was it like this, Comrade Dimitrov, the great
rehearsal of 1923?)[2]

"That's terrible! Get back! There's no enthusiasm!"
shouts the commander of enthusiasm.

And
the revolutionary
armies
meekly
head
backwards,
their fists dangling.

The commander of enthusiasm is in despair:
"Akh!
It's easier to have a revolution
than a parade!"

[2] Georgi Dimitrov introduced Stalinism to Bulgaria in 1947. The "great rehearsal of 1923" was Bulgaria's first Communist uprising, inspired by Russia's October Revolution. When the uprising was brutally crushed by the military, Dimitrov fled the country and did not return for over two decades.

Dog

Why do you watch me so sadly and inquisitively,
friend of 16,000 years?
How can one repay such lasting friendship?
With a bone, with bread crusts, oh, you don't want bread,
                    a piece of sugar then—
or some other scraps from my lunch?
Or shall I pet you—
after which I'll have to wash my hands?
Or whisper endearments—
at which people would laugh—
and you—would you even understand them,
friend of 16,000 years?

Listen, dog! Come—
we'll read some Bradbury together,
concentrate, set aside all your other thoughts,
don't look at the table, please,
          concentrate, and like the yogi
who conquered gravity by mental power
and levitated eighteen inches off the ground—
concentrate,
levitate,
start flying . . . (I know it's impossible,
                         I've been struggling myself for years,
but no luck . . . Try, and I'll hang onto your tail)—fly!
The night is clear, Mars is on the horizon, the moon is at its zenith—
                    use its gravity, fly in a parabola . . .

If you can't, run away!
Run away to the forest and live without sympathy.

When a Poet Is Born

—to Miriana Basheva

When a poet is born
Heaven opens
its old gate
and God kneels humbly at the threshold—
a new universe quickens
when a poet is born.

When a poet is born
the executioners seize
their rusty axes
they spin their grindstones, they hum happily—
executioners don't lack for work
when a poet is born.

When a poet is born
Socratic skulls
smash open their coffins,
blow reveilles on vertebrae and shinbones—
for resurrections loom
when a poet is born.

When a poet is born
the bells in their hearts
rouse the children,
they dress up, rush around merrily:
Is it a wedding or a wake
when a poet is born?

When a poet is born
only mothers cry,
they veil themselves with the dusk,
stare in horror at the empty cradles—
for themselves they've created nothing—
when a poet is born.

untitled

The old woman leans against the pine tree
and looks at the treetops. She's crying,
but her eyes like limestone soak up the tears,
they soak up everything. She has no more illusions
that anything might happen—falling in love,
giving birth. Old woman,
all that remains for you is to die—
the last human adventure.

And this thought is vast as a sea,
and you're only one of the fish
that can't escape from the sea.
Come on, don't cry.
Say good-bye to the treetops, to the birds, to the wind,
                    to the ants,
                    to everything;
only to the earth say, See you soon!

She's waiting for us, a whole life she's been waiting for us,
the earth, this dark Penelope—
a couple of eras back she let go of our hands,
now she's clasping us by the feet
and we, unfaithful little Odysseuses, are trying to fly,
and whether we manage to or not, the hour
of the great landing will come . . .

It's getting dark. The old woman leans against the pine tree.
Far away from cares, far from money, far from things,
                                        far from our battles,
the halo of her hair shines in the dark,
she cries under the stars,
above us all.

Nostalgia, or A Painful Return to Memories

A city forsaken by its dwellers,
a city wracked by an invasion or some treachery,
dead city, city for two, city of one street, one square, one
bench, or a city of one room plus one moon—

No,
don't go back,
you won't find what you're looking for,
don't dig for coins with your old, forgotten
image on them—
we overvalue relics . . .
How incredible we are:
Caesars, Cleopatras, Krums,[1] Pericleses—
and how much more incredible with our simple names!

All else has been preserved:
the street, the square, the bench, the room, the moon,
(like a magnifying glass held up to what we lived)
we're the only thing missing—what an affront!—we scream but no one
replies—feelings die before people, all else has been preserved:
a city reinhabited, a city well rebuilt,
a city minus two.

[1] One of the pagan *khans* of the early ninth century, a famous conqueror.

Nikolai Kanchev

Born in 1936. Nikolai Kanchev is the author of more than ten books of poetry, most of which were major literary events and subjects of controversy due to their condensed and sometimes obscure metaphorical language. He is renowned as a translator of poetry from French and English into Bulgarian (Henri Michaux, Yves Bonnefoy, Kenneth White, Gary Snyder, etc). His works have been translated and published in the United States, France, Holland, Italy, Poland, and the former Soviet Republic of Georgia.

Seventh Heaven Can Be Seen at First Glance

He who sleeps on his palm
cups his ear to hear
a voice from other worlds.

But even here, noiselessly,
the turtle advances
so slowly towards death.

And I so wish to live
just as I am now, not
for an instant outside this one.

Those who gaze through telescopes—
what use peering through the keyhole
of a stranger's home?

A Smile

Summer's last thunder: and from the treetops
flocks of birds are soaring toward the sky
like leaf fall in reverse.

And there's nothing strange in this, let alone
frightening, since somewhere, with a smile,
an old man is waving at the lightning bolt.

And as autumn starts, the soul,
one naturally assumes,
has a leaf fall such as this awaiting her.

Birthplace

And what if time were to stop?
The end, no doubt, would be surprised.
The house on the hill where you were born
is waiting for you to rebuild it.

How, and with what—bricks of clay and straw?
You remember only the chimney,
the smoke vanishing as it spiralled
like a kite string

dropped from heaven to earth.

√ **Glory**

The sky with reddened eyelids foretells windy weather,
fleeting things ready themselves for anguish and extinction.
But look: the thorn itself is crowned, and none the worse—
and you are like its shadow, ever sheltered.

But nothing so grand occurred while you were living,
deaf, until this day . . . and is it because
the house in which they baptized you is scattered
dust, and slowly, slowly, everywhere, your name is spread?

Church

"I've come to kneel before you, while you're falling down,
I'm not crying for your damp walls,
nor for the saints' moist glances.

I can't utter a word above you,
I don't know what you're for, nor how to ask.
You're bound to place a cross, an end, on everything."

"Without me it will always be as with me.
The sun will remain in the sky for you,
and the lightning bolt with its will of light.

And as for the essential thing, why ask
whether it's tragic if here on earth
you're more than a building with a building's fate?"

Feeling

It's raining as if for the first time—
what's wrong with me?

Nothing I compare it to
is fitting.

It all was ruins, what lay basking in the sun.

What's past is past,
but look at this:

The masons of new worlds
are holding plumb lines.

Miracle

Disquiet issues from the clouds—omens for us all—and at night
the watermelons shine so red from within they even
light the way for the moon, that it might emerge from the deluge dry.

How its rays are rattling, as if a fevered train
were writing in the distance on a broken typewriter, and a robin
dashes towards it like a red signal light

But what salvation in the monotone prayer that uplifts us,
the hill with no sense of its own weight rises up with our bodies,
and the dog is running toward infinity, which tosses a cloud for it . . .

It's a miracle, the waves' effortless procession on the water,
a miracle, the word that they're not the deluge . . . whatever
life may be, the earth twirls with joy on its Achilles' heel!

Binyo Ivanov

Born in 1939. Binyo Ivanov's poetry is some of the most innovative to have appeared in the 1970s, with its startling imagery and subtle allusions to folklore. For years his writing was ideologically suspect because of its occasional obscurity. Ivanov has published four volumes of verse and has been widely translated abroad. He was an outspoken political dissident in the struggle to dismantle the totalitarian regime.

One Can Rest

One can rest in a war.
Jagged smoke-cables tug each other, a horse is dying,
the silence rusts
on overturned trucks,
on bullet-pierced helmets.

The barbed field
staggers like a wounded duck, stumbles in a hole
at every step, tangles in jutting roots, while
sand, damp pebbles, and a few tiny monocles of ice
rain down on it.

It reeks of fried beams, mattresses,
photographs, diapers; and nearby
butterflies and combs, and a bundle of letters are hissing
in the flames, and the letters, riddled by a pair of eyelash rows,
are blown by a ball of dizzied air onto a torso frozen above a well.

Your patched shirt, the dried-out buttons,
are smoldering on your breast
(where one is missing, a thread-tip blackens),
iron filings shriek beneath your feet,
houses, towers, bridges with straining walls
are dying in your eyes.

An endless mouthful crumbles on your tongue,
the bottomless sacks of your pockets
feel like drooping wings, the lines on your palms
are all minced and kneaded with the muck from crawling,
feathers sprinkle your hair like confetti:
you sit, eyes half-shut, in a ballroom that hasn't danced enough.

The directions are jumbled, but on one of them,
far away, close up, between some branches, your home is swaying:
a fence, if it's not ash, if the ash isn't blown away by the wind,

if where it's been blown to is left in peace,
if it's not already dust,
if the dust, at least, *is* dust,

you sit, you chew the rusting silence,
at peace beside your gun, your finger crooked, the clocks
are all clattering, the duck staggers—falls, falls—staggers, clattering
until they all begin to chime you to your feet and on your way
toward the hot earth.

A Tale That's Not a Tale

It
tears us whole:
maybe green,
maybe overripe,
from the familiar branch.

I snowed
seven feet and a hut for you—
in the center a hearth's teeth,
overhead a candle gulps wind,
outside a wolf sings and stops to lie down,
you watch me in the fire, the forest
is swelling with wolfsongs, swallowed wind.
Maybe green, maybe overripe . . .

far away, close up,
a crowd many-faced and familar throngs,
gestures, shouts, overwrought:
they're crazy to have run away into the forest!

Otherwise
it's forestlike outside, human,
slightly dark,
already late,
very near, snowy and melted;
three smiling children, they're ours, gaze at me,
or at you,
as you slip through your wedding ring.
And
you're gone:
I glimpse nothing of you and the fire,

only
the wolf's tongue licks me and speaks to me and shines to me
that
the world's wide and white,
I didn't believe it till today,
the whole snow has fallen and is heaped to the sky.

Summer

On this long farm facing Rila Mountain,
filled with tobacco carts,
my father's grave is ripening.
On this long farm facing Rila Mountain
where the sun bathes twenty villages
with twenty houses each,
where the river that had set out for fish
disappears at the edge of a melon field.
The hills head east,
three dry shrubs on their foreheads,
they're thinking of becoming mountains;
on their wide way
my father's grave is ripening.

His friends have forgotten him,
mother's forgotten him
and I'll forget him soon—
but the sun looks on,
the tobacco grows sturdy and bitter,
the melons puff themselves up,
soon a colorful ant
will emerge from the slab
and say, "It's ripe now!"
In a while the market will be laden with
heaps of tapped and chiming melons
and bulging tobacco bales,

and the hills, their foreheads blazing,
will keep on heading east.

√ **Bulletin**

It's not a good sign
when ministers of war are in a hurry.
It's not a good sign
when generals eat on the run.
When soldiers march
night and day
it's not a good sign.

It's not a good sign,
my bud of something.
Be cowardly,
be scared to death.

Frightened branches—
listen for the wind.

Look around you, roads—
stretch your gaze far ahead.

Night, listening into your depths,
be our calm.

Wary
dawn.

Cautious
day.

crickets, green-faced

stretched-out
tensed-up
dug-in
between stone-roots
they break
the silence
doggedly
swallow it

floods
wars
earthquakes

they warn us of it all

A Man

And so, when my core cried out
that it felt everything was upon it,
I cast a bold look as far as the sky,
through magpie nests
and reinforced concrete.

With my eyes bulging
as if I held a knife to them,
I cast a bold look as far as the sky
through feathers and twigs, through the holes
in my children's, and everyone's unconcern,
through my wife's, and everyone's pain,
I looked, I understood.
I looked, I understood
and saw the time I've spent hanging around
in the evening
in the morning
at night
without memory
without weariness
          doom
          strength
without churchbells
without guitars
amidst grinning beards
          and eyes that forgive the innocent,

to the edge of the shore, to where the ocean begins,
where it ends, till I turn gray (all too obviously),
till my bones start to creak and my hand repels me
so that I can take neither crumb nor knife from it.
I looked, I understood.

And it roused me, this boldness of mine,
to walk among creatures who put bread in their mouths,
enter the cinema, watch, buy (don't steal) macaroni
and on holidays, cabbage, comforted, comforting,
with their tickets, their justifications for every moment, every coin,
with windows and curtains, creatures
(and among you, wasps, bumblebees,
                doves, cats,
                minnows in lazy lakes,
                slender branches, spiderwebs,
                a pebble from heaven,
                from space,
                some higher civilization
fallen at my feet.)
I looked, and understood,
I looked, and understood.

And suddenly my thoughts collected themselves
                and returned beneath my hair.
I blocked out my whole self with the palm of my hand
                in my shirt
                on the chair
                beneath the hoarse briars
                out at sea.
I folded myself up, set myself aside without a thought.
a tree trunk all efforts and tendons
running fearlessly,
noiselessly on
so as not to disturb anyone,
not to give myself away through the thick windows where
the creatures with their justifications breathe, eat,
they eat like creatures with seats, with tickets, usherettes
with foreheads bent toward their flashlights, with breasts
that have sprouted buds for bees, hornets, drones, with thighs

between which sweetness itself—that most scrutinized
of creatures—finds its place, naked and alone,
secure and naked.

I folded myself up and set myself aside,
I stepped over myself, the earth was calm,

I was approaching, approaching, approaching.

The Wind Is Coming and I Love You

The wind is coming and I love you,
dawn lifts an arm, the sunset fades,
a cloud is drying and I love you.

You, sunstruck dust-speck, droplet
dripping from a roof-tile's beard,
a single letter from a letter from a friend,
a maiden's lip, a mother's grief.

A pale, pale old man sits on his fur hat.
On three Balkan mountains bears he stalked,
on three Balkan mountains bears he skinned,
to have it growl on his uncombed head
in his eternal wars with vermin.[1]

Yantra-fish crawl from the Yantra toward the Danube
where fish in bulging nets speak
thirty-three languages.

A gold-bearded she-goat climbs
Mount Musela's rib,
clouds butt against her horns,
dying to set the sea on fire . . .

The wind is coming and I love you,
a cloud is drying and I love you,
I'm scattered by a surging
in your lakes—a dream beneath my palms,
by your grasses' udder,
by the roosters on burning roofs,

[1] This word in Bulgarian also means *pagans*.

by chimneys that scrawl
long greetings on your skies.

The wind is coming and I love you,
a cloud is drying and I love you,
when I lie down I embrace you whole,
you, dust-speck that entered my eye
for a tear, sun that lights my road.

Ivan Tsanev

Born in 1941. Ivan Tsanev began the new wave among younger Bulgarian poets of what was called (first derogatorily, then admiringly) "quiet lyricism." This movement grew out of aesthetic and political opposition to the April Generation's occasional extravagances and ideological concessions. Tsanev has published five volumes of verse (including a *Selected Poems*) as well as translations from Russian and Hungarian. His poetry has been translated and published in all the Eastern European countries.

An Archaeological Site

—to Ivan Teofilov

In the center of town, on the small square facing the mosque,
the stream of people stopped and pickaxes started clanking
—a new sewer maybe?
Before the passersby's astonished gaze, stone steps and bleachers
emerged day by day.
At first we'd stare at them in silent wonderment—
centuries ago, the gladiators' blood
flowed scarlet on these stones!
What dramas were once played out here . . .
But when our curiosity was quenched,
the small square turned back into an arena
of provincial, rainbow-colored life,
untroubled by the ghosts of history.
The ice-cream vendor repitched his pavilion,
and once again a joyful crowd rushed and clamored
with childish disrespect for the ancients.
Sic transit gloria mundi—thus the world's glory passes,
said the Romans themselves, with a smile.
Only the quotidian is eternal, it seems.
Are the living to blame because breathing intoxicates them?
A procession of baby strollers makes its way
past the stadium's magnificent ruins,
and I hear the town echo with the triumphant cries
of little warriors who, this spring day, came and saw and conquered.

Note: The ruins of this Roman stadium are a famous landmark in Plovdiv. Only a small section of it could be unearthed to avoid tearing up a major downtown intersection; even so, part of the modern commercial district was rerouted to accomodate it.

Express Train

A sudden green gust from a roadside tree
just raced the length of your gaze.
Did you see it? The driver's sly smile
has remained behind the bend; he spurs his dusty
little truck down the jagged, bouncing road.
How unexpected the windshield's glinting
in the sunlight just a moment ago!
The multicolored kerchiefs that painted
the landscape have vanished,
and the women's voices, ruddied
by the afternoon, have faded out.

And there, on the hill, almost
in the sky, a whitewashed house
dawns like a mirage,
like the house in which you dreamed
you were born. And you're sure
that if you'd spent your days there
you'd now know what perfect happiness is . . .
The tow-headed boy who, with a comically
solemn gesture, waved the train on its way,
has disappeared from view.
His freckles melted in the sunset.
Dusk is thickening and copper sheep-bells
clamber down the slope,
a pack of big dogs, ears erect, rushes
after the caboose, and the engine,
as if frightened, runs even faster.

And again trees, hills, people, houses
rush past you—gaps
through which you peer

into another life, more intact
in its apparent chaos. And outside
the stations, the lamps' yellow lightning
spurts suddenly from the darkness, then dies.
The train rushes headlong, its wheels beat
against the rails, hammering in the night
the iron melody of your journey.

Bee

Red-headed laborer streaked with soot, your buzzing fills my ears,
Isn't your fragile name like pollen stuck to lips?
You unify the particles, breathe sweetness into things,
and I see you circling between branches like a pensive ray of light.

Bound by the finest thread to my delighted glance,
you climb higher and higher, each flower a step for you;
the ultimate selfless caress, you say good-bye to the white tree,
you cover the silenced day on your tiny humming path.

What treasure do you guard so zealously in your simple hive,
with your urge to hoard that's never satisfied?
I know your banquets are your hardest workdays among the vines,
you tawny sweat-drop oozed from the amber grapes.

Your wings, sister of my diligence, spread the scents of honey
and hurt all around, and it's becoming ever harder to reach you;
if I should try to stroke you, you jab your stinger instantly—
and it's the rootlet of a song for you, falling bee!

√ **Cricket**

Your tune trickles on as it has always done,
and along the July cart-tracks, through the chapped grass
your unnamed path cuts across the yellow stubble-fields
(and who knows where it leads).
Seeds and clods trip you, but absorbed in yourself,
you play for summer's banquet. And each evening my sated soul
is lifted on high by your fixed song,
before falling sound asleep.
But in your orphan's dress, sewn from dusk and dew,
why do you live always in the dark, hidden from all people's eyes?
(I now realize an adolescent's irony resounds
in your unpitying, helpless voice.)

—I can't stand words. As soon as you're asleep in your bed,
I exit the night . . . and I listen to its moments ring.
And everything I see through the slits of the stars,
day slashes with a golden scythe.

Fine Day

What have you kept looking for
in the dark, what lost thing,
while so many years passed by,
as though slept through,
in a windowless house?

But a child came and called you:
Come back to life's warmth, look
how many laughters
are chasing each other in the sky,
when you've had your fill of gloom
you'll come along with me,
and we'll go count the rays
in the sunflower field.

Koprivshtitsa

When we'd climbed the panting hill
and the tiny church at last opened
its carved gates before us,
the icons' eyes burned in the half-dark.
And it seemed to us that coolness wafted
from their severe, self-absorbed glances,
and their silver-chained hands,
in dumb accusation, invited us to kneel.
We became silent, suddenly estranged.
Then the shrine spoke up; we heard a voice
(heavenly? earthly? spirit or man?
determined to reconcile, through words, life
and saintliness) tell us:
" . . . these are the very saints who
once, that memorable, mad April,
removed their halos and donated them
to the saints' conspiracy . . . "[1]
Hadn't we just heard the most Bulgarian of secrets?
In this enfevered land even prayers
taste of uprisings, and flamboyant deacons
climb to heaven from the gallows;[2]
the monastery was once a rebels' inn,
and onto the icon stands and carvings sifts
the dust of unbridled roads.

Note: Koprivshtitsa, an historic town in the Balkan mountains, is now preserved as an architectural museum.

[1] In the "April Uprising" of 1876, the Bulgarians attempted to overthrow the Turks, who had occupied Bulgaria for five centuries. The reprisal was a massacre that led to the Russian-Turkish war of 1878, in which the Turks were finally expelled and the Bulgarian state restored.

[2] Ex-deacon Vassil Levsky, hero of the struggle for national liberation, was hung by the Turks in 1873.

Ekaterina Iosifova

Born in 1941. Ekaterina Iosifova has published six books of verse and has produced some of the most lyrical, reflective, and spontaneous poems of her generation. She has been translated and published in all of the Eastern European countries as well as in the United States, Italy, and Greece.

March

I'm going to your fair.

I'm going with my worn-out skin, my five-year-old raincoat,
and the field will be swarthy, the sky bright blue.
On this much-walked road my feet are happy,
and if I set off on time, a pink mist will shine.
        I'll tread a path which
        isn't worth a cent, can't be bought for gold.
        I'll find the root of faithfulness
        and the flower of the unchatty mouth.
I'll hide my hundred tongues
and only try to listen in
on a nightingale's throat,
on these muddy hills, ugly as pregnant bellies,
where future grapes are swaying.

Vast is your hand—
you have days for me once again.
Vast is your hand for me and for others.
Violets smell for one and all,
a tiny rumor is hopping
on islets
of last winter's grass
and a quiet rain for those who pass and those who don't
is both a consolation and an unaccountable tear.
Vast is your hand—perhaps I'll manage,
at the last moment, to pause under it.

At My Doorstep

As I was standing, not even at the window,
simply standing between pot and plate,
contemplating my next three spoonfuls,
I sensed someone waiting outside.
Evening was falling, shadows
rose from the ground and filled the air
while I stood on the doorstep.
Perhaps it was a child
who was waiting,
perhaps a man
who had to hide his shadow
(in such a peaceful homey night,
when all shadows are acquainted!),
perhaps it was a woman,
whose jealous soul
was shrieking like a bat nailed for good luck
to the door of someone's passion . . .
perhaps a star was burning.
Thus I lingered at my doorstep
in this homey, peaceful night
when all shadows are acquainted.

If the Silence Should Suddenly Return

What will call out to us then,
children suddenly awake
because the clattering cradle
which lulled us
has stopped rocking?
Shall we hear the same night
embrace us in turn,
the same dust
as it's crunched between our teeth?
Shall we think: if only it were freedom
that divided us!
Shall we give one another confidence
like dwellers in a peaceful home,
as if we'd made a pact
to come always to each other's aid?
And knowing each other just through rumors,
shall we start talking to strangers?

If suddenly the silence should return,
will that chorus of hushed voices
invade us,
or, utterly deaf to the outside world,
shall we listen inwards
(if our core isn't dried stiff
as unreachable larvae eat it hollow)?

If suddenly . . .
But there are no savior-miracles,
the silence has been long dying,
we rock in our cradle
while our youth alone goes leaping,
a squirrel amidst smoke branches,
a fish caught in nets of screams.

Nightfall

Shadows dart, the wind has risen,
the river has stopped reflecting the air.
If you leaned over the darkened water now,
you'd perhaps spot the eye of a doe
who senses danger in the bushes
yet still bends down to drink.

River, this moment's alarm
courses only in the blood which resembles you,
while your voice flows equally clear.

When everything was still the future,
bottomless water, I used to cross you up to my knees, and—
when a falling star struck the night like a flint—
in my pure heart's vast ignorance I made a wish
for everyone on this small boat to take pleasure in their days.

I'm standing, the only witness
to my only life.
The river bends at nightfall,
someone catches sight of his old shore,
a face appears,
a fragile light dissolving
into dusk.

The Cloud

It's darker and cooler—
the great cloud is passing between me and the sun.
It's traveling fast, the far edge
of the shadow will soon touch you.

What are you doing now? What will you do tomorrow?
The days melt like clouds.
I thought I'd grow old
with my forehead next to your shoulder.

I might dream you, might sleep for a while
untroubled next to your big body.
Untroubled beside your smiling soul
(I say this with a smile).

It's wide and quiet here. No one changes his life.
The cloud
will pass.
Ahead there's nothing but the coming night.

Beneath Winter's Roof

Let us honor the offerings,
let us chop quinces for the wine,
let us bring out memory's salty grapes.

Yes, it's been wonderful,
we experienced all we could
(which wasn't so little, after all)
and pain is joy's companion.

The heart's ageless love song—
that priceless game that can overturn all verdicts.
We'd wake up ready for joy,
for we were children taught we'd be forgiven.

We tried out a scream and all kinds of silence,
all kinds of words—the earth's big enough,
we won't weigh her down—
or we could even keep silent like old friends.

Wonderful world, where
the most important questions go unanswered,
where the sweet wells don't run dry,

and the future
will be no less vast without us.

Nedelcho Ganev

Born in 1944. An outsider to the literary scene in Bulgaria, Nedelcho Ganev has been almost completely uninfluenced by poetic trends or schools of thought. His distinctive voice, fresh and full of startling metaphors, has strong supporters among many of the leading poets, although it has yet to find wide public acceptance.

Matter ✓

My soul was created from matter.
A small amount
            but endless.

Familiar
            but unfathomed:
When I step toward the fire
            the flames, like widows,
            scarve themselves with smoke.
A river flows through my body
            but I remain thirsty.
I join day and night with a welding torch,
            but the separation won't close.
How can I speak of charity
            when they cured me the folk way
with live doves' hearts?
I used to love riding bareback,
            but they broke me with an iron bit.
I trusted the young maple,
            but it wound up an ax handle.
The source of this poetic disorder lies in my chest.
It carefully
rearranges sunsets and people
strata and colors
and it's from this motion that life quickens.
And should it die out
even verse will start to cloud,
and flames to waver.

The Soul

The flame is full
of thick tree-shadows.
In it shrivels
the forest's soul.
I gaze at the fire
and the light's morse code transmits to me:

The flame is your life:
Burn small
and you'll die out.

And this:
The flame is your life:
Burn big
and you'll quickly turn to ash.

Small green devils
leap over the fire like kids
and play with it.

Height

Through the cut poplar I can spot
underground rivers.
From some torn fur tufts,
the she-wolf's lair.

I can drink up the wine
without it touching my lips,
try the tip of the flame with my tongue.

The earth churns,
            it rhymes with a boiling pot.
            Viper-tongues crack against heated stones.
I stroke the sun's gold coin in my palm
yet I'm clothed in tatters of cloud.
What height!
I thin out the flocks of birds,
I roll the lightning bolt's hoop.
An unbeliever, I slowly sip the heavenly wine
and my song fades into color.
What height!
Even eagles get dizzy up here.

I don't know how else
to keep the petty ones at bay.

Further

They took the stallion out into the field
and struck him with the whip.
                                        His hooves
tore up the earth as he broke into a gallop.
Because he was sick they shot him
at the end of the meadow.
His hooves continued beating
beyond the river.

The drunk leaped up from the table
and smashed the musician's violin
over his knee. The violinist
continued drawing his bow
                              across the invisible strings.

Leaning his forehead against his walking stick,
the old man dozed in the sun. A mischievous child
approached and pulled the walking stick from under his forehead.
I cried out. The old man
                                  didn't budge.
He continued dozing, his forehead leaning on his sweet memories.

The Verb

A calm wind blows
and lifts up the eyelids of the verb.
Everyone's waiting for it.
The bridge—a cat's leap—
arches its back so time can pass.
The murmur of the forest
touches that of the heart.
A yellow onrush of crocuses
clogs the cart path.

The verb settles the worries of the dead
in our blood.
It paralyzes the executioner's raised arm,
fans the fire in the blacksmith's forge.

Without the verb the phrase is dead.
And the green twig amidst the surgeon's instruments
has no one on whom to operate.

Boris Hristov

Born in 1945. Boris Hristov's lush and unflichingly emotional poetry has made him one of the most popular living poets in Bulgaria. He has published three volumes of poetry, novellas, and a novel. He was a visiting writer at the University of Iowa's International Writing Program, and in the fall of 1990 he gave a reading tour of the United States. His poems have appeared in the former Soviet Union, Poland, Hungary, Czechoslovakia, Germany, Austria, Italy, and the United States.

Evening Trumpet

Life turns us beneath the scorching sun
    and we wear down our feet against the hot stones . . .
But when evening drops from the skies I'll fetch
    my trumpet and sit in the doorway.

Enough of wandering around these walls
    like the ringing of a punctured bell.
I must play, I must tear down
    the silence—so that only the cry remains.

I want the hot wind to thunder
    and blow all doors wide open.
I want the earth to follow once again
    the crickets' crusading march.

I want to rip with my song
    the barbed wire around your house.
I want my neighbor who deafened himself
    to regain his hearing.

I want the thief to bind
    his fingers, the guard to buy himself a heart.
I want to drop some of my tears
    into the rusting eye.

I want the fair to return to us
    and blow away the dust.
I want those who are dying of boredom

to die of laughter and tickling.

I want us all to keep vigil by the dead
until dawn comes.
I want to say to all sleepers
that there's time for us to sleep well.

I must play in the deaf evening
until I hear the nearing voice
of a thousand far-off trumpets.
Or an invisible archangel.

The Window

I stand on tiptoe to reach the window that's open a crack.
Behind it are the women—rounded by the steam, beautiful,
How I want to see them—if only I could climb up the wall,
or if my friends were here to lift me!

How the women frolic and chase each other—
they remind me of a herd invading the sunset . . .
And in what mold did God cast their breasts,
that the swaying should be audible even in the street?

A red ant is creeping up and sometime around noon
will reach this view and die on the window, with hazy delight;
Again I stretch up and claw at the wall—
like water thrown on lime, my body churns within.

In my life I've always reached the windowsill—no further.
And then, I can hardly catch my breath.
And there's no one to lend a hand, no one to rechannel water
to the dry land where my hope is gasping like a fish.

But I'm torturing myself in vain! Who helps us
see anything—here, in heaven, or in the infinity of art?
Why do we so often ask who among us is the poet?
And why, one behind the next, are we standing on tiptoe?

My Mother's Wedding

He climbed down the hill and went off somewhere—
my father slowly sank into the green grass.
I've been waiting for him for twenty years,
and for twenty years my mother's been courted.
Men come with fine footsteps,
sad and lonely, carefully combed,
they speak, they offer her their hand,
but she doesn't want to know . . . content,
she steps outside, busies herself in the garden,
goes off, returns with a pail of milk,
sits on the doorstep and chats with the silence.
It's been this way for as long as I can remember.

But one day the groom will come,
and the three of us will sit in the room,
quietly clarinet will whine,
our souls will be still—we won't speak.
His hands will arrange the crumbs, she'll watch him,
and at last they'll start discussing their health.
Our little house will revive
and I'll go away and leave them.
My mother will weep for a while in the doorway,
then slowly she'll lie down
next to the unknown man's kind shoulder
and my dead father's heart.

Solitary Man

He has a scar on his forehead and always sits apart.
Even when he's tall the solitary man is small.

He gathers herbs, or with the penknife of his memory
carves something if he's bored, always dragging an old blanket.

A horse's skull lies gleaming in a field, and the solitary man
goes up to look at it, not minding that it doesn't have a mane.

While others shout or talk about art, the solitary man
sits at the table, catching and releasing flies.

But if he wrote verses he wouldn't fail to leave
a tear in your eye or a scratch on your memory . . .

He has a home and he has hot soup, but his life
is secluded as a crate discarded at a hallway's end.

And if the house were ruined, roof-tiles to the ground,
he'd eat ashes, but he wouldn't plead or beg.

In what fire he has burned, under what iron,
you'll have to drink a lot of wine with him to learn.

And as he walks, a spot on his clean shirt,
he's suddenly lost in the crowd like a bead.

In one hand he carries a book for sick souls, and with
the other, in his pocket, he clenches a piece of rope.

Dandelion Bone

The sun has its lunch. It loosens its belt,
drinks its wine, its neck is flushed.
It pours down on me—but I won't remain
a specimen preserved in this day's alcohol.

Outside, life splashes and roars.
Though a funeral procession is about
to pass, I'll clutch my hat and say there's
no such thing as death (there couldn't be).

And even if I die, I'll reappear
in the sparrow's eye and watch you
from a tree, or with a haughty beetle's walk
I'll cut across our neighbor's yard each morning.

I'll be the thistle accidently
stepped on, the cricket hoarse
from the mist, or else the bramble
that toys with a lamb's curly tail.

I'll be the mouse running with its young,
exhausted, along the prison walls,
the dandelion listening through its hollow
bone to all of nature's pain,

I'll be the words that await me
on a stone (death can't conquer words).
I hear the bone of the dandelion growing,
I hope that you might hear it too someday.

At Night

Our tree's shadow is green at night
as we hurl our bodies against one another,
and like a thief disappearing in a prison's mouth
I lose myself behind the gate of your breasts.

A thousand steps into the night, far beyond the hill,
someone's weeping wakes the silence,
Death, broad-shouldered, approaches him
but we're unmoved—distant death is a stranger to us.

They're liars, who feign tears for the man
at the end of the world, who don't want to know
that just outside in the street two other men battle,
or that a knife's already lodged between the ribs.

Now that I've known life to its last tooth
my arms can embrace just one person.
I meet the dawn watching over her as a baker,
face flushed from the oven, watches over his dough.

And what does it matter if solitude says,
"She's the gleaming ax whose blade your finger tests . . . "?
Until I've melted like a lump of sugar
I'll go out in the night with a lantern to find you

And I'll fall in the mud, but with flower in hand,
and when death's glider snatches me up
I'll be waiting for you on heaven's top floor
and there we'll decide where to go.

A Sign from Heaven

The rain smothered us, the hail
swept up every living thing into a ball.
I saw God's ice-carved head
fall from the sky and land in a field.

While its forehead still glistened in the cold noon,
its soul was slowly steaming out,
I picked it up as one picks up a lamb
and my solitary voice poured into the silence:

"Tell me, Jesus, you who left the flock
of Judaea weeping on the hilltop,
you who let child and hangman alike
into heaven after Barabbas, the evil thief,

why crucify man between this mud
and sky, roasting him beneath the starry fire,
why make the poor widow Earth
a vast blotter for tears?

I'm no prophet, yet I can hear
through my Bulgarian skin
your blowing on the horns of the Last Judgment,
and the knife touching bone.

Tell me why, like a conjurer, you hide
in the torn pocket of the dark abyss
your hand which is ready to grind our blood
to dust and drive us out of here forever."

But God just looked with moist eyes
toward the hill where the cross was glowing . . .
and while wondering what to say to me
flowed out in drops between my fingers.

Georgi Belev

Born in 1945. Educated as an engineer, Georgi Belev worked in that field for eight months before turning to a career in literature. Since 1976 he has published five books of poems, ranging from satire to lyrical nature poetry.

Tale

A children's poet's own child is dying.
Such a crowd jostles around him—
wise owls, talking mushrooms,
noble ladybugs, the foolish wolf,
the comely fox, keen and cunning . . .
they've all amassed, and wait.

A children's poet's own child is dying.
Absurd snails slide over him,
their cool slime slowly transforms him
into a piece of mica, yellowish and brittle.
A raven is swooping to snatch it up
so it can shine forever in her wing.

A children's poet's own child is dying.
"There's so much air in here, why did you take it all?"
—the shaken poet asks his creations.
But the steaming mob doesn't hear him,
it churns and reeks, impatient
for the end so they can all run off.

Dream

When the trees began to calcify, and the birds to coalesce with the branches, and the moss to turn steel wool, when transparent beasts thronged from all sides . . . you tried to run away, like last night and the night before, and once again your feet stuck to the earth that stretched like gum beneath them and you felt breathing and gnashing against your nape. You screamed, you fell back on your drenched pillow . . .

Beside you your mother slept, your father slept, everything slept in the stifling room; anxiously you rubbed your soles, but nothing . . . and already the moon's head on the curtain was guiding you back out of the forest, and suddenly you're in the sunshine and the air wafts wonderful mountains—ice-cream cones—toward you; you step forward, small and eager, to receive them—but the rocks below await you, you slip and fall—and your words soar up in flight.

Woman

Weeds loom—
trees huge
above your head,
you nestle,
a small beast
discerning each smell,
a passing ant
dragging another
(perhaps the two of you
have crushed it).
The man over you
is just his shoves,
his face
is far away—
a moon behind clouds,
now it shines,
now darkens . . .
You feel the coolness,
your skin tautens,
you tell yourself:
He is young,
a little scared,
you feel his cheek
gently scratching your palm,
a whizzing comes
from the road
followed by darkness,

the cars chase
their own lights
as you'll chase this moment
for years.
But for now
you gather sensations
like a bee lured
deep into a forest.

Love

What do you scrawl
on my back
with your fingernails
at your moments
of greatest weakness?
Sometimes
it's the tender circlings
of a bird above her nest,
sometimes, alarmed
by her young's ravenous
cries, you sink your claws
into the bristling fur
of a rabbit fleeing
down a barren slope . . .

A child.
The steaming prey
for the child. And nothing else.

Zoo

In their cage, the lion mounts the lioness.
Their muzzles face the crowd. Wives leap toward the lioness' eyes, squeeze through the flaming hoops of her irises, and, arch-backed, try out the male's weight.

In their cage, the lion mounts the lioness.
The men, grasping sons by the hand, grow smaller, and the sons grow up—they're fathers now, they ask no more questions. And the fathers are boys—how they see, hear and remember everything!

In their cage, the lion mounts the lioness.
He withdraws, she sprawls, her paws flash white. A hot stench rises from her belly, reunites the families and sends them off. Their bars clang shut behind them, and just a brief roar rattles them from within.

√ Lake

The blue woman climbed out and kissed him.
The boy rose and slowly undressed,
oblivious to the stones that jabbed his feet.
A bird wept and flew away so as not to watch.

His chest skin bristled finely,
she laughed, she stroked him,
found his lips again and drew him into her—
the coldness stung his groin.

He turned and gazed back to shore
but the reeds were thick black smoke
and the frogs had built their cries into a wall.
Stay!—she said, and squeezed him tightly.

Gleaming lake—on whose bottom
huge fish fatten, motionless,
their mouths outgape each other
as the water-mother drops something in.

Train

The wind stretches fields,
night trails towns and clouds
and gaping railmen's booths . . .

The boy's awake now
in his window seat,
it's his life that clangs and whistles
down the endless jaws.

And the windowpane reflects
a pair of shifting faces,
now a boy's, now an old man's,
and a star above them flashes
then fades out.

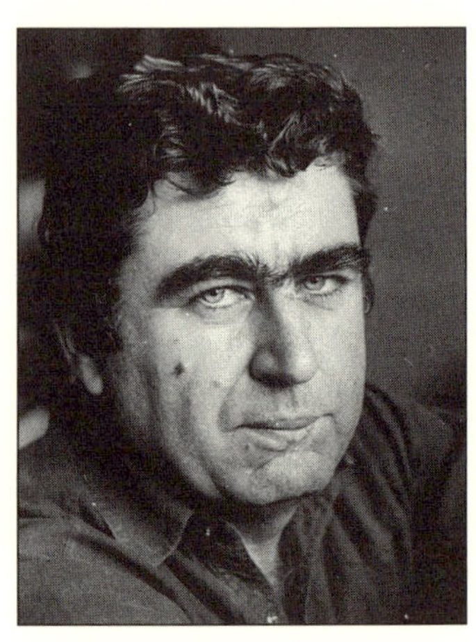

Marin Georgiev

Born in 1946. Marin Georgiev jokingly refers to himself as the last rural poet of Bulgaria. His credo, masterfully implemented in his poems, is that the poet should be the soul mate, not the opposer, of his predecessors—even as far back as the anonymous folk poets of centuries ago. Georgiev's first book appeared in 1975, and he has since published four other books of poems as well as critical essays, nonfiction, children's books, and translations of Russian poetry.

II

> ***" . . . a man, even if he lives well, dies, and another is born; and may the last born, seeing this, recall those who made it . . . "***
> **—from an inscription on a column dating from the ninth century reign of Khan Omurtag**

> ***"History relies mainly on the regular multiplication of the human family; the most important world events should be traced to family secrets. Our ancestors' marriages give us cause to reflect . . . "*** **—Goethe**

Heads beside roots, pressed against them, you sleep.
Nerve fibers web their way through the earth.
Oh, I'll pull you out by your hair now braided
with the grass and weeds and bushes—
isn't this your tears, the juice that rolls down the stems?
Rise up, dead ones! Like an unempty womb
you weigh me down—food, fur, sweating backs,
bodies sunk to the depths of the earth. Wheat is sprouting.
I eat of the bread, but it says nothing to me,
I've drunk of the water—my lips quiver, unquenched, try to speak.
An ant, subterranean messenger, crawls across my fingers,
rushing to return, mute, to the earth.
Mist rises from this fallow land,
like your last breaths above the damp clods.
The sun struggles to burn through it.
A hoarse rooster. And smells and sounds.
Then you melt with the light.
The haze spins a web above the pastures,
red-yellow spots play before my eyes,
grass, leaves and vines are tripping me.

This and the following three poems are from *Memory*, a cycle of 15 poems.

V

There, far away
in impassable forests
behind nine rivers and mountains
where the age-old bearded
eagle flies,
there, amidst the dead leaves,
the all-curing spring wells up.
A hundred-year-old stag
drinks the water,
clear and cold,
and digs at the ground
with his hooves.
His crisscrossed horns
are like the wreath
on the wiseman's head,
he hears everything,
he knows everything,
for everything he has a cure.

Blow on your finger!

It's passing, isn't it?
. . . Because *he's* passing by our house,
the stag, the stag,
the forest-czar!

That's what my grandmother used to sing,
how she cured everything,
clenching a handful of flour.

And now, before I try to break
a chunk off the steaming loaf,
I'll wait till he's gone full circle
around the forest and field.

VI

With her evil yellow eyes,
for months the plague had been circling.
She would soon enter the village,
and neither barking nor fire
nor woodcutters' axes
would scare her away.

So . . .

Two twin brothers
with two twin steers
with a wooden plow
(from a forking elm)
plowed a deep furrow
far, far away,
around the village,
making room for the fields,
making room for the graves,
room for the dead, for the living,
room for weeping, for love.

May folks multiply, and cows
and grass and wheat,
and may health never end
like the waters of the River Vit.

VII

In delight, at the moment of conception,
our blood churns, dizzying us.
Our bodies swelter, tremble,
hairs on end, veins burning.
Dry-mouthed we give inaudible thanks—*Mother!*—
just as in our greatest sorrow,
our most unbearable pain.
Prone, spent, again we whisper her name.

The root of sorrow and joy,
anguish and delight, is the same.
But our mothers have long been in the earth,
beside their own mothers and grandparents,
underground kin in countless rows,
forever stretching out their hands in love or hate.
Moles tunnel through their hearts,
and the worm, merciless sentry, guards their kingdom . . .

And aren't our cries and moans
drawn out along with our body's
juices, our souls crucified
by birth and death,
by endings and beginnings . . .

And isn't the insatiable earth,
giving and receiving,
in fact our beloved mother
to whom we pray, exhausted?

She hears everything,
and comes to fetch us.

Silence

In the afternoon hours of autumn heading home,
beneath the cooling sun which had paused to light us up,
picant moistness squirms soundlessly under the stones
and herds of shadows pass before the gates.

Your sigh threads long from your lips
and the small cloud above the crag rounds out and grows.
The child from the mountain village plays with fire,
and you can sense the spider making a web in the clearness,

the sap sinking down to the furthest root,
an anthill boiling over late in the dry grass,
and the gypsy summer[1] clover watching it,
gingerly advancing towards its fourth leaf . . .

[1] Indian summer

Riverbend

At its bend the river thrashes,
splashes, hacks at the shore.
At its bend, the willows swill,
the hemlock sprouts, and nettles and reeds.
Shadows trudge through sinewy clematis,
weeds grow thick and pungent.
Fish leap in the coolness,
water snakes weave around the roots.
Icy centipedes dart,
sated worms writhe.
Mortal odors of decaying young green.
Black flies buzzing, enraged.
Earth and water. And between them slime.
Clammy, sticky,
everything's veiled in blue mist—
what's being born? What's dying?
Slippery tree trunks, water
and darkness coalesce,
it's always dusklike and frightening here.
Is this the dark river floor or an owl calling out,
and the voice—is it song or sob?

Native Soil

Begrimed by trains,
deafened with words,
pressed by people,
how I'd love to shout
Get lost!—
to wipe my face with my sleeve,
to rebecome the boy I once was,
a bee buried in a blooming poppy's pollen.
Everything's a burden, all of you are burdens!
Where are you, sun—
and you, sky, cleared by the wind,
rainwashed.
Insatiably I gulp down air
sweeter than the tears
of first grief.
Let me sleep, a walnut tree's shadow drawn over me,
with my arm for a pillow,
gnats buzzing around me,
ants crawling over me.
I'll sleep this way for months
and awaken like an oak tree in the field
that hasn't felt itself grow,
that wedged its feet into the earth
and its head up there into that white cloud,
to stretch my massive branches to the cracking point—
let the gales whoosh, my crown will barely stir,

and everything will be a first for me.

Ivan Metodiev

Born in 1947. Ivan Metodiev was educated in science and worked until recently as a research chemist. His relatively late debut in poetry revealed a mature and original talent, and his recent work, inventive and well received, shows a playful and wide-ranging intellect.

River

River, River,
tell me, River,
what are your children called?

They're called fish,
and they're called frogs.
The first ones gleam, the others croak,
the first ones gream, the others cloke,
the first ones splish,
the others frop!

Are you going to want
another fish?
Are you going to want another frog?

Tell me, where is my fish,
tell me, where is my frog,
tell me, child,
child me where is it,
fish me where is this tell,
where is this where—infrog me!

I'm here—
I'm your fish!
I'm here—I'm your frog!

What are you saying, child—come to your senses!
What are you childing, what are you whatting?
Have you ever seen a frog with a sack?
Have you ever seen a fish with a braid?

This and the following five poems are from *Songs for Orphans Big and Small*, a cycle of poems.

It's one thing to braidle, another to fishel!
You'd better not froggle
in this gleamy fishness!
Now stop it, child, don't cry, go away—
you're somebody else's,
I don't want you!

These Things from Words

Tell me, Moon—
what's a Tramp,
what's a Ragamuffin,
what's Getoutofhere, Moon?

Your mother's not here, child—
I know these things only from words . . .
Your mother's not here, child,
she became a willow,
she became a river,
I know these things only from words.

Tell me,
when a small orphan grows up
does he become a big orphan, Moon?
If he grows really big
do they make him King of the orphans?
Do they give him a golden pillow?
Do they wrap him in a magic robe,
tell me, Moon!

Your mother's not here, child—
I know these things only from words . . .
I'm still new here, child,
I'm not yet a quarter full.
Come and take one of my beams
for a blanket.

This Crow

This crow is unlike the others.
The shine of shards doesn't appeal to her.
This crow can clearly make out
the diamond's inner world.

But when she sees a diamond, she doesn't get carried away,
she simply says—here's a diamond!—and leaves.

And her caw means—
here's a diamond!
here's a diamond!

(As does, by the way, the caw of all crows.
And therein lies this crow's misfortune—

that she sees through to the essence of things,
yet she's robbed of her essential cry.)

This crow carries nothing to her nest,
the shine of her feathers
is enough for her.

Garden of Questions

Three old men in a scrawny rain
on a backdrop of blooming pumpkins.
A scarecrow. A bird is digging
in one of his eyes. On the hill, a snail.
On its back, a tiny house.
And in this house
two clouds head north,
and three wet rats head south.

What Is can be clearly seen—
the rust on a cross,
the breath of a turtle,
the salamander, half-risen,
his tail still in God's dream.

(Though this may be unclearly said,
it happens that for God this world
just happens to happen.)
And it happens that a beetle flips
and rings in the mud and scratches the sky,
that under the sky there's a small yard,
and in the yard a young pine tree,
and that beside the tree Peter Piper's
picking pickled peppers.

Since God is eternal,
God never happened.
(And for what has no beginning—
though this may be unclearly said—
it happens that nothing ever happened—
and it never happened
exactly in this way).

Sometimes

Sometimes God resembles a kitten
whimpering under the moon.
Sometimes God becomes the rain,
sometimes a rain-whistler.[1]

Sometimes God resembles nothing,
and sometimes the nothing becomes God.
And the wise person's goal is to choose
of two empty things
the fuller.

But God is Alpha and Omega—
therefore God is round.
And the fact that Judgment Day is coming
keeps enlightenment away.

For
all sides of the Ball
are only Left or Right.
So on which side of God shall we stand
on Judgment Day?

Not God, but you yourselves, will judge you!
And this, in fact,
is your Sentence.
Judgment Day will have come
when everyone's a judge.

But tonight God chose to be a kitten—
he feels like licking the moon.
And sometimes God is the whole kitten
and sometimes
only the tail.

[1] A bird, known as the golden-eye in English.

Sonnet-Mantra of the Crickets

After each drop of rain—
a different silence.
After each drop of rain—
a different silence.

After each drop of rain—
a different silence.
After each drop of rain—
a different silence.

After each drop of rain—
a different silence.
After each drop of rain—

a different silence.
After each drop of rain—
a different silence.

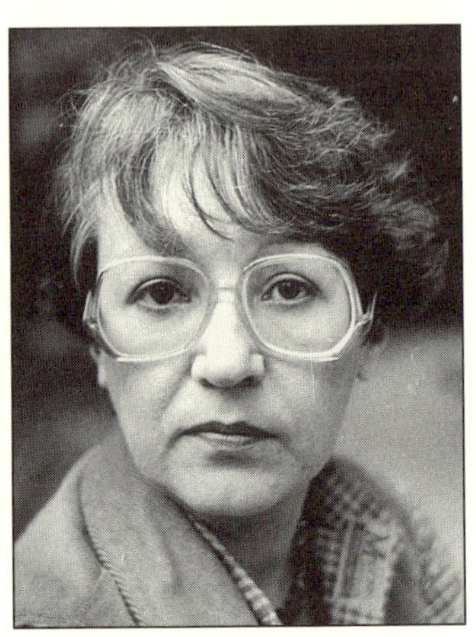

Miriana Basheva

Born in 1947. Miriana Basheva is the daughter of the reform-minded foreign minister Ivan Bashev, who died under mysterious circumstances during the 1970s. Her first book, published in 1976, was a sensation in Bulgaria with its sharp, ironic style reminiscent of Marina Tsvetaeva. Her work has been widely translated in both Eastern and Western Europe. She has published only one further book, in 1980, and her poems now appear infrequently in journals.

Morning

Where was I last night?
—Stefan Tsanev

Where was I last night? In whose arms?
I remember only some lips beside my heart.
I remember palms prowling tender and cruel.
I remember—"More! Let everything in you hurt!"
I remember the rain dripping down my back.
(It was no more than that. It was not a man's tears.)
I remember the long good-bye, the short walk home.
And I fell asleep like a cat lonely to death.

untitled

The fast train? The express?
I waited, smoked, turned male.
Curses hissed in the dark,
it was raining like hell.

A dwarf archipelago's
semaphore twins
pierced ocean puddles,
waved trains to the wind.

In despair and alarm
the green signal burned
as did I, while a cop
pestered me for a light.

A sad-muzzled pickpocket
circled a coat pile.
On all lords and all thieves
in the world the rain fell.

And on me. I'm still waiting.
I've turned male from waiting.
It's bucketing down
on these crazy black trains.

Rabid steam whistles
through clenched, wicked lips.
It's raining like hell! On all
stations, all men in the world.

N.N.

I remember you, Comrade N.N.,
with adoration and respect—
you were so young! So married . . .
I, for my part, studied. Got top grades.
(I studied different things
under my desk—Madame Sagan[1].)
I was your small but faithful dog.
But you didn't whistle. And haven't till today.

It was like before the 9th.[2]
Or even before Christ.
Your veto was loud and clear.
Good evening, Comrade N.N.,
I remember you. *Bonsoir, joie.*
Now not so young? Unmarried?
Still a Don Juan, just as before.

But why, contrary
to the normal course of events,
do I shrink to a child's dimensions
in your huge arms?
Just like back then—without my homework
in front of the school gates—
I'm scared speechless,
I can't bring myself to say
your name.

[1] Françoise Sagan was a French author whose novel *Bonjour Tristesse* was written while she was still in her teens.

[2] The Communists took power in Bulgaria on September 9, 1944.

Fifth Floor

Existing is not always appropriate,
yet it's already happening to me,
on a daily basis.
Should I tell my doubts, "Nothing doing!"?
But they'd miss me . . .
And I, them.

Damn these long poetic nights,
that stretch from here
all the way to there.
In summer they display them in full force,
they broadcast them through fountains over Eagle Bridge.
And (how shall I put this)
they make me howl—and not just once—
silently at the moon from my apartment
on the fifth, top, floor.
It's a good thing
people are deaf to silence.
As well as to cries, by the way.
Some bricks nearby respond
and engage my fingernails in battle.

It's on nights like these,
crumbling around me
with all their concrete weight,
that I discover, in some antiquarian volume,
the traces of lost time.
The poet went looking for me.
But
he didn't wait around.
Maybe it's better that way.

Life's a contemporary performance.
What dead genius would understand me?

And despite everything
I slip between the lines,
almost painlessly
like a knife-tip.
And—
a hundred bronze men sit down beside me,
to come to life with me
for at least one night!
The floors merge into a warm house,
a real river bursts forth beneath the bridge!
Lost time is restored to me,
I'm almost sure
that's the case . . .

Dawn breaks all around.
Finale. Curtain.
We'll survive tomorrow.
(This crazy life . . . !)
A casual night episode
was hanged on a sunbeam.
And the dog, always first up,
is deftly watering the yellow pavement.
What nice thing will happen to me
on my way down
from the fifth floor?

untitled

If before they smashed my jaw, now my
whole soul is drenched in blood.
—Esenin

Not long ago a whole sun
plunged into the sea—almost without a sound.
It grew evening-cool.
Just right for a white suit.
Instead of a shawl, elegant night put on
a swarm of constellations.
And under my fine, feminine skin
a coarse soul was shivering.

She recalls how many times
we've hid beneath pink makeup.
Oh, my soul,
it's more than children's games
going on behind your back.
You know how gracelessly I limp away
from every lost battle.
How planet-sized chunks
stick in my throat.
I see how hard it is for you,
with your male temperament,
to have to walk only forward,
like a pawn—and behind me.
We both recall the cost
of our utterly French finesse,
the plaster on the Louvre—
and the price does us justice.
We'll daub on a little more paint
the way others spice up their jokes.
And behind this contemporary skin
there's only meat to be seen.

It Was War

Red horses
trail their bridles.
The slaughter was fierce.
Their riders are gone.

In iron heat
twin tanks burn down
like requiem candles.
Their scrap is gone.

Clouds and fogs
of poison prowl,
just as if
the planet were gone.

The moon dims,
anemic-faced
like a woman
whose love is gone.

You think, moon,
they're still calling you.
It was war.
They're all gone.

Georgi Borisov

Born in 1950. Trained at the Maxim Gorky Institute for Writers in Moscow, Georgi Borisov is a highly regarded translator of Russian poetry. His mastery of form and the dramatic force of his poems reveal this Russian background. One of the chief editors of the Bulgarian journal *Fakel* ("*Torch*"), Borisov, along with Rumen Leonidov, was responsible for the first publication in Bulgaria of censored Soviet works that surfaced during *perestroika*.

The Horse

Up the moss-grown,
flood-steep path
I walked, while he made
his slow way down.

His naked back gleamed
like a dolphin's amid the rocks,
his cracked hooves were sticky
from his journey and his blood.

And against the high wind
his golden skin trembled
like the embers of a god
who remained alone on earth.

I stepped aside to let him pass,
and caught a glimpse
of his branded flank . . .
I did not look back again.

And high up, beneath the mountaintop,
I saw twin crates full of bread and wine
and on top of them, frayed twine.

I drank and ate all winter long.

Ravens

Lonely birds who cross out the sun—
why are you circling toward us?
To snatch the worms' food,
to sip water from skulls,
to bathe in blood?

Crucifying the sky on your wings
and shredding the air on your husky squawks,
oh, are you birds, or a spell
the winds cast
on my road, on its white snow?

Why do you hover and fly overhead,
why this bristling of your flocks?
What dark mourning do you ordain,
whom do these sinister screams curse?
Are we one footstep short of death?

And alone in the earth's heart, where
root inches toward root—
I hear the snow arching
the trees, and the winds
stalking you, and destroying your nests.

What Freedom Said ✓

The bird carrying the wind in his wings
and the wind carrying the bird away,
the tree gnawing at the earth
and the earth with the tree tamed in her jaws,

they're equally free: the tree will be a bird; the bird, dust,
and I'm just the man standing between them today.

Gates

These people on the road—why they've gone out,
where they're heading in this fog, I don't know,
since in their tall house behind the iron gates
they've left the dead man alone.

He lies bareheaded and unseen within,
his puzzled eyes are wandering.
My God, he says, everyone here is dead,
what use are these gates to them?

untitled

And when the winter wind rushed straight into my heart
and the wolves' centuries-old howl resounded in my throat,
and the night peered at me, her glance bristling and mad,
I got up and cursed the night, my blood, the sun.

And I slipped noiselessly through the peaceful city like a beast,
beside hotels and hospitals, taverns, cars and shops,
and I saw the last kerosene drops blooming
like blue poppies on the wet, black asphalt,

dead neon moons suspended in street corners,
the last lovers walking in the dark gardens,
and I heard the maternity ward echoing with songs,
the last trains whistling their sharp farewells.

And when I reached the middle of the deaf, black field
and the earth's salty blood licked my palms,
and when overhead the last snow began to fall
and heaped the night, the furrows and the muddy road,

the wind carefully swept my tracks,
its swirls wove an icy noose around my throat,
and the earth was hanged, and my body swayed
like a last song under the bright, sharp stars.

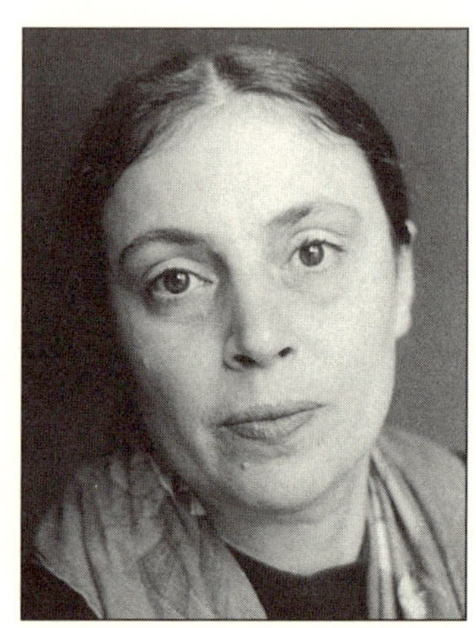

Fedya Filkova √

Born in 1950. Fedya Filkova has published three volumes of poetry and more than ten books of translations of German and Austrian fiction. The unvarying briefness and delicacy of her poems is unique in contemporary Bulgarian writing.

Vulnerability

I.

Without fear,
I take off my loneliness.
Full moon,
come lie in my womb!

II.

Your love brought death—
so there was no pain.
The angel lingers
uselessly above me;
even the stroke of its wing
is a blow
after you.

III.

May the summer cure me of this love
that peers at me with dead fish eyes.

IV.

The day is vast in my tiny room,
halos gleam from my favorite books,
an open peony peers at me from its vase,
each sigh is a bridge that leads to infinity.

Arrival

Did you hear
the tulip burst open?
—A peaceful salvo
for your arrival.

Friendship

Death gives way sometimes,
especially in August
when the nights are still short
and the darkness has much to get done . . .

Then even crocuses shine in the fall.

Under a Wing

Voices play at will.
The words are robins that take flight,
catching up with others
as others catch up with them.
No one minds the game.

The silence smiles.

Frost

A hospital garden on Sunday.
It's midsummer and I'm sitting
with my mother.
Her lips on my forehead
are the familiar hot compress,
but she, twiglike,
is shivering all over from the frost.
And I sit with helpless hands.

Buchenwald

Retribution keeps watch this summer day
and smiles with a hollyhock's innocence.
The dead, were we able to revive them,
would refuse us who are still the same.

Rumen Leonidov

Born in 1953. After his debut as a critic, Rumen Leonidov published three books of poems. His grotesque and caustic style was for many years an obstacle to the publication of his works. With Georgi Borisov, he founded Fakel Press, one of the new small presses that are flourishing in post-Communist Bulgaria. This press has published, among others, Konstantin Pavlov.

A Stone in the Swamp

The stone's finely wrought parable
ends with a plop!
And the circles of life start rippling
and dissolve in the silence.
The stone's finely wrought parable!
The water turns over in its sleep,
rolls from its left shoulder onto its right
and
some
flying
frog
lies
down
in its bed of slime.

Another Stone in the Swamp

—A translation of K. Pavlov

The stone
I threw in the swamp
turned into a frog.
And started to sing
with the rest of the frogs—
also former stones,
thrown
by another naïve soul
into the swamp.

Misery ✓

Because the straitjacket was short on me,
they put me in a knight's boots.
They stuck a headpiece on down to my eyes and chopped
off my arms, just in case.
And because since then I only meet knights,
I rush to shake hands with them

and sometimes I get away alive.

untitled √

The mouths of the people eating their lunch
the mouths of the people eating their lunch
chew,
they're careful not to spill their soup,
chew
so their main course won't get cold,
chew,
thinking about tomorrow's dessert,
which
they love, the people eating their lunch.
From their chins to their wattles to their thighs
hangs
their word,
but the people eating their lunch
catch it
in a napkin
and the word crackles like a bug
which surprised
itself with its own jump toward them.
Themouthsofthepeopleeatingtheirlunchkeepsilent!

Vladimir Levchev

Born in 1957. A well-known dissident (despite his father's official post), Vladimir Levchev founded Bulgaria's first independent literary journal, Glas ("*Voice*"), in 1989. Educated in art history and criticism, he has published six books of poetry as well as volumes in translation by Allen Ginsberg, Odysseus Elytis, and the first full-length verse edition in Bulgarian of the *Bhagavad Gita*.

Four Seekers of the Great Metaphor

I.

He understood that words are living beings.
He dwelled among them and with a priest's fervor
helped them love one another and lie down in nuptial metaphor.
He aimed to unite them in holy societies . . .
But away from the pure fields of his temperate parish
he lacked the ruggedness to bear the savage,
sweating bodies—in that tropical country
each holy impulse burns like a useless sheet of paper . . .
While here among his yellowed manuscripts he was the doctor
to whom the skeleton is dearer than the man.

II.

He rejected empty words. He loved the fullness
of wine glasses, women's breasts, town squares.
He knew that here on earth, and not in heaven,
one must undergo the great metaphor.
Life alone has meaning! Paper is empty!
Live and drink—breasts, liquor, bright skies, sour cherries!
He drank up his days, sucked his memories dry,
then emptied his hopes, drank still more out of boredom . . .
At last, awake and sober, he realized: Yesterday I killed—
and his life-verses were a metaphor of death.

III.

He didn't think about his bread or distract his mind with wine,
he himself was the bread and wine of life.
He didn't sacrifice his time to books,
he himself was a read and doomed innocence . . .
He signed his name in heaven with his crucified flesh,
he crossed out death, illuminating it with human sense,
he made out of his own flesh and blood a metaphor
to sow goodness in barbarian fields . . .
If you cast the merchants out of your inconstant spirit,
the man in you, though crucified, will still live on.

IV.

Sometimes His eye is like a moon
that fills our darkness with maternal sorrow.
Sometimes, blinded by His anger,
soaked in a sweat of thought, we lug our mortal burdens.
Sometimes a star will burn above the sunset
and an eternal secret breathe in tired forests . . .
Just as each parish deserves its priest
and each wine smells of the winemaker's soul
and the kingdom is a wayward dream that troubles the king
at night, so the landscapes around us portray their Master.

Athens

Later that night you find yourself in someone else's house—wooden ceilings and cupboards, a smell of oldness and olive oil. Beneath a flickering red lamp a woman, kind and tender, half-undressed in the sweaty sheets, gazes at you. Drowsy men with feverish yellow eyes are talking in the room. The woman awaits you. Her eyebrows meet, and there are black nests in her armpits and between her thighs. While you wait anxiously to be alone with her, the woman's face shifts. When it's the green-eyed one, with the body of sunset and sea-breeze, you remember her, you love her . . . When it's the one with the black eyebrows, she winks at you and shows you her heavy breasts . . . Sometimes she laughs like a nervous boy, and you hear the owl that sees in the dark and feeds on the mice of madness . . .

Outside in the hot green night big snowflakes start to swirl. It's August. Strands of multicolored bulbs and Christmas ornaments rattle among the tall masts. The sea has flooded the city, bringing in the ships from the harbor. Already someone's crying for help. In the snow outside a body's heat arouses you. The woman with the changing face stands naked in the wind. Disaster looms exultantly. The woman stares at you in silence, half-opening her soft lips. You take the pulse of the frightened bird in the black nest. Thighs embrace you and the sea enters.

Now do you understand why Socrates so willingly drank the cup of poison two and a half millenia ago?—The owl's beak shattering his skull was a lover's kiss.

Blue Pond at Berkovitsa

—to Tsvetana

We swam naked to the blue pond's shore.
But it had invaded our senses.
We had a long climb up the sunless hill—
the chill at dusk inflamed our bodies.

Far away on the road I saw us walking.
But the road led into me.
And the fire in the yard was more than smoke:
the stars singed me as I fell asleep.

On a damp sheet on an antique bed
I entered your dream then.
Now it pulses on my forehead,
makes love to my naked soul.

The desk and the lamp—a circle of light
in a churning mountain stream . . .
A scent of pine and snow and menace,
down below, a blue dusk prowls.

The faded summer wafts from the grass.
It smells sweetest when newly mown.
Warmer and nearer is the blue sky today
beneath the cold, black firmament.

The moon is mute and red. It resembles
this evening a widening wound . . .
Life, open, bleeds and drains.
The world's death is one that lasts.

Beacon

—in memory of Danila Stoyanova

In the gale, in the field's bright stubble,
the bright scilla, eye of the nothingness,
is so vulnerable it baffles the lightning,
a bolt drops, stones burn,
the red-hot sycamores sizzle . . .
the scilla observes,
itself becomes the blue sky.

Sky—serene and fragile flower,
brightened by magnetic storms,
breathing in the darkness, blue atop green,
it flickers, blooms, fades,
witnesses the death of stars . . .
In the blackness of the cosmos
who blew the sky in and planted it?

He who loves all transient things—
a ray of sun, each conception,
the history of the earth itself—
he'll be as small as the tear
that brims in your eye
in the storm of an eternal farewell,
a flashing beacon in the sea of death.

Georgi Rupchev

Born in 1957. Author of several volumes of poetry as well as translator of American poets Robert Penn Warren and Lawrence Ferlinghetti, Georgi Rupchev (along with Miriana Basheva) is one of the most highly regarded of the "urban poets" (so-called because the city serves as the backdrop for and defines the inner life of their poems). Rupchev is equally at home in classic and free verse, and his poetry is characterized by its psychological subtlety.

Ceremony

They'll be here soon, they've already been called.
They'll be here soon—we're waiting.
Orange flowers interweave above our heads,
hissing like Chinese dragons.
And we're sitting as we always do around a circular table
sharing a moment of headache.
Born to pass on our life and blood,
we play our inherited roles.
You who are on your way, why aren't you here yet?
The clocks' hands pass through eternity, pierced our souls,
which flowed out hastily, thick and uncertain,
and time rushes deafeningly by.
And all our lives we've stood up and sat down,
stood up and sat down, endlessly, with dignity, with our birthright,
receiving and receiving again, chatting vacantly . . .
They've already been called, they'll be here soon.
And look, they're entering the room,
and look:
They're taking away the duchess, half-draped in an orange blanket.

Stand up—make way for them,
stand up
so they can lead the madwoman out.

Reversal of Worlds

It continues to the edge of the mirror
and there reflects and vanishes.
He might often have walked around the room,
tidied in vain.
His turntable might have spun empty—
and the world, like a worn-out tune.
The tenant might have gone out sometimes on the balcony,
peered down from the twelfth floor,
the clock might have ticked, the coffee boiled,
and the wind might have foraged through the open pages,
the sky might have changed its paint—and he, his shirt;
he might have played with his tomcat, started in his sleep,
and this evening he probably would have had a long smoke,
listened, seated in his armchair, to the radio
watching the fog come down from Mt. Vitosha,
and the wine he slowly sipped would have tasted good to him . . .

This is the room, the bed is made. Beyond the wall
the city is silent. As is infinity.
A silence which was left behind, in his haste,
by the departing tenant.

Still Life

A cello on the bed—
like a body expectant, naked.

(In front of the piano,
bought for a song,
you, bow in hand, were the madonna and child
between the candles, breathing over the keyboard,
and you thought the neighbors would get angry again,
I was still there, bewitched and unrecovered;
outside, the December buses had been rumbling for an hour,
and the mournful "A" crawled between us
huddled against the picture of Rachmaninoff,
the wardrobe creaked, the walls began to moan,
a subsonic mass for all saved souls,
the morning poked through the blinds like a neighbor,
I hadn't yet put on my sweater,
I was probably smoking and thinking of music and so on,
relaxed, I listened to and watched your legs,
the coffee pot, the clock and the steaming cups,
a nightgowned musician was seeing me off.)

Attraction

Prostrate from the heat the earth withdrew,
the sea congealed, we went far out into it,
the fog, with red tentacles, rocked
the beautiful fish and furtive medusas,
the sky lifted before us, colorless and full,
we cut the motor,
we cut the motor and the silence encircled us,
the morning grew, interlaced with our muscles,
its claws stabbing our backs,
it roared in our ears, gripped our chests,
and we dried off, happy and alone . . .

Then my friend stretched out on the floorboards,
shielded his eyes with his palms, turned fantastic,
I passed him a cigarette, we lay there, still damp,
lay there, creatures of dry land, sunburned, skinny,
we smoked and steamed in the haze, in the shabby boat,
we spat into the sea which bloated around us,
in the heat between us flickered vaguely
a half-sensed peril.

Bewilderment

We were many in the room
    and, like a drunken cartman's whip,
a woman's laughter slashed
    against the halted silence.
Her moist nostrils trembled
and on our smooth backs
spilled the pain from the whip and a sharp
shudder from future hours.

She cursed us, and slashed again:
Giddyap!!—
    Dear God we should have galloped, but
we stood frozen like Akhmatova's first adolescents—
timid, ardent and, for no reason,
a little remorseful.
    For the last,
    for the first
    time—
as though chiseled, almost perfect,
    hobbled,
ready to die if necessary.
A different blood was making the rounds of our veins,
for the last and the first time.
    And on our other faces the colors were changing
    and with tentative gestures we changed our faces.
Were we really fading, too tired
to be men?
So we stood—docile, silent,

hooves wedged into the unbridled earth.
We'll be this way tonight.
For the last and the first time.

Danila Stoyanova

Born in 1960. The first of Danila Stoyanova's poems in *Clay and Star*, written at the age of sixteen, can be seen as prophetic of her death seven years later of leukemia. Her poems were collected and published posthumously in 1990.

untitled

They say I don't love life.
That I love the dead tulip not the breathing one,
that I'm in love with the sob and feel only
                                                  the laughter of the sarcastic.
That to the sun I prefer the rain and the electric wind,
that in the raging spring I seek out pre-ordained tragedies,
that I take the shroud for something sacred,
that I recognize man only in his animal wisdom,
and that shoving with the mob intoxicates me.

—
Oddness, or deception?
—

I only know my funeral
                              won't take place
because it's hard to bury someone
who puts death on a par with life
and lives equally in both.

untitled

Three mares
at night,
diluted by a rainstorm,
gulp the coolness
in such great throatfuls
they melt
in the dark.

Lightning bolts cleave the moon
without making a sound.

Everywhere a mare's back
and wind.

untitled

—to my friends, to their
despair and hope,
I dedicate this.

the sea woke up
after a night of nightmares
filled with fish and seaweed,
whales and medusas.

You're leaving,
and in your legs are rippling, coiled
and sticky, the memories
of their words:
— . . . your clever forehead,
your beautiful face . . . —
They sink like craters into the wounds
from their innocent thoughtlessness.
Your smile is blind,
like their blind eyes.

The lonely, nearby sea . . .
you lay down beside him
and surrendered to his cold hands;
whispering and white the surf crawled up,
engulfed your body,
took you in his afternoon visions
to rock you, and he kept on
rocking you.

Tonight the sea
fell asleep with your nightmares,
and its waves were heavy and slow

like delirious words from underneath thick quilts
covered with sponges and soft seaweed.

— . . . your clever forehead,
your beautiful face . . . —

They remembered you
that other afternoon
when the sea came lonely and near,
they looked underneath the sea,
leafed through it,
and in the clear green water
some people, white and drowned,
were swimming amidst streams of sun.

Ani Ilkov

Born in 1957. Ani Ilkov's poetry, at once whimsical, quirky, and obscure, is already among the most original being produced by Bulgaria's younger generation of poets. Although his poems have been appearing in journals for years, their experimental nature delayed until recently the publication of his two books.

A Scene

She's crying.
She steps up on a cloud,
she's awarded the moon.
A gorgeous blond
with hair in profusion
(it's in black and white,
this blackness and whiteness)
our evil passion,
our evening star.

She's cutting her hair
in front of a mirror.
Naked—she's wearing
only her body.
The man is eating
his supper at the table, sullenly
eyeing the splendid woman.

(We know: she's had other men.
And will have! The sun lowers
a rope,
climbs down to see her at night.
Her name's golden,
embossed
on night's skin . . .
The sun loves her—
she loves him!)

And she's crying—without clothes.
The man eats his supper.

She's cutting her hair—
evening star.
Day's last rays.
Her hair falls.

It will rain.

Of Stone

Balkans and Balconies—
I'm suspended
My absurdities have no other goal
They want to sing to themselves
and be heard
in Dobrudja[1] and Greece

A Bulgarian soul—
the dried-up cats that flip-flop in your dream
like horse carcasses in the incinerator at the end of the village
If someone dies or September
crucifies the grapes on the vines
and takes them under escort of the rain
toward the heavens—
in other words, if they rot

I can rhyme or not
But it makes no difference
The stone won't hear me
The coming night won't hear me

A Bulgarian soul—forget the letters
A Bulgarian soul—the blood, the blood

This poem is from *Orbis Tertius*, a cycle of poems. *Orbis Tertius*, which means "Third World" in Latin, is also the title of a story by J. L. Borges.

[1] A large, fertile and much fought-over plain that straddles the Bulgarian-Romanian border.

Ram

When young I lived up to my chin
in grass.
I didn't feed my name with glory, but day
by day
my hair grew lower and lower,
and higher and higher grew the rays of gold poetry.
My father, my mother and my dead relatives,
standing next to an oak or peach tree,
refused to embrace me with love,
wouldn't listen to me at all.
"Why," I asked, "don't you want from me
what I can give back to you?
I'd lay under your feet even my shirt
of linen,
even my own spring fleece.
If I wanted to, I could kick thunder loose from the storm,
I could make the mountain speak!
But you keep living your gloomy days
while the joyful ones you wastefully discard . . . "
Thus I grew up with my poetry—running
down hillsides I overtook all the people,
I was the first to arrive at the grape harvest
and only my grandfather bound
my neck and my innocence with wine
as red as sacrificial blood.

In that hour under autumn's knife:
"Don't!" I said to him. "Grandpa, my skin
in Trifon Zarezan's[1] clay dish
will turn golden brown.
And your grandson the Ram—you'll never

[1] Patron saint of vineyards whose festival each winter celebrated the trimming of the vines.

catch him in the tall grass,
don't raise your knife!"

What was that experience in life's dawn?

How I learned that first autumn,
that Death would let me write poems!—
and the grape seed would be the period,
and the grape leaf a shield for my joy,
best man and witness of my final stay of execution . . .

I was lost amidst the sap-filled grass
in the costume of an animal sacrifice for our sins,
but when the grass had finished its silent yellowing,
I leaped naked from my own skin

and saw:

sprouting on me hard, evil horns,
I was taking part in the motion of the spheres,
and, myself the blacksmith of my own destiny,
I headed springwards, sunken in the snow,
and then in Aries, in the Zodiac, I found myself.

Dreamsters

The scary thing:

We dream our ancestors
and they dreamed us long ago.
And that's why we sometimes meet in dreams
and live together there like close acquaintances.

We plow the earth in moonlit fields,
and from the wheat of our native tongue a voice is heard.
Fogs and minds multiply,
animals and names evolve . . .

It comes time to separate from our ancestors,
but we're already so alike
that we can't tell:
Are we all just waking,
or are we all asleep?

Muses

Listless, still, they seem to weep,
they've ringed the willow trunk
and their palms play with the branches.
The river flows away and they'll

find consolation hard to come by.
(They're lonely because they're invented:
but no doubt because they're lonely
they're alive.)

Idylls—gauze-like, transparent—
in autumn they travel to Egypt,
and a peasant tramp installs himself in their place
and dozes off like a seed beneath the earth . . .

Now it's still early but the willows
are already trembling—the nights are cool.
And fish and petals quiver
in the cold water and the bluish air,

the sky-shepherd is milking the stars
and a chorus of gray spiders chants:

"Lazy-white and lazy-pale
by all mind forsaken.
O, ex-muses, sick and old,
to see you weep we're shaken!"

River. Star. And grief . . .
. . . —drying leaves.

Green and Gold

Man's a carnation,
woman a vase.
I'm the petal
on the rim of the vase
on the windowsill.

Now:
the ancient leaf
shivers proudly—
the vast sky is above,
Homer below.

Now:
the Byzantine leaf-tip
is golden.
It's embellished with mosaic and silver
and somehow suggests the crucifixion.

Now:
there's me—
a poet, an artist,
smelling of earth and heaven,
a crumpled leaf.

Now:
Man is a carnation, woman a vase.
Chlorophyll is wafting from the lamp,
a green man has started crawling on the table.

Evaporations

Warm, living flowers
are thirstily awaiting
rain and poetry,
a grasshopper will leap
from green to pink,
and down through the yellow
another color is descending:
everything turns multicolored,
everything turns sudden—
like a snake's quick arc
in the grass.

An instant before I chose my name,
a rain fell and washed away the letters.
I leaped up to see
why the grasshopper had leaped before I did.
And I came upon words that flew in the sky,
emptying basins of water and legends from above.
Higher up the rain is warmer,
that's why names there always become vapor.

A Peony and a Lion

A lion with peony eyes
and a peony with a lion's mane . . .
I was standing in the field
and thought it would be impossible
to yank a scream from a flower,
or feed nettles to a lion.

But great things are sporadic and lawless:
The flower roared with its petals
and the lion caressed me with his claws.

I ran off and wrote this down:
It could be that an unpaved road exists
toward what we think the mind can't reach:
a lion with peony eyes,
a peony with a lion's mane.

About the Translators:

Lisa Sapinkopf was born in 1958 in New York City. She studied literature and translation at the University of California at Santa Cruz, the University of Iowa, and Boston University. She has translated the complete works of the French poet Yves Bonnefoy as well as Brazilian and Portuguese poetry and fiction. Her translations have been published by some of the most prestigious literary journals in the United States, Great Britain, and Canada, including *Agni*, *Boston Review*, *Boulevard*, *Paris Review*, *Partisan Review*, *Pequod*, *Ploughshares*, *Poetry*, *Salmagundi*, *Stand*, and more than two dozen others. Her translations have won the American Translators Association Prize, the Columbia Translation Center Award, and the Robert Fitzgerald Translation Prize. She lives in Cambridge, Massachusetts.

Georgi Belev has translated Robert Bly, Galway Kinnell, Mary Oliver, Adrienne Rich, and Anne Sexton into Bulgarian. He has worked as editor in charge of literature in translation at Narodna Kultura, one of Bulgaria's leading publishing houses. His own poems have appeared in journals and anthologies in the United States and Canada including *Boston Review*, *Nimrod*, *North Atlantic Review*, *Paris Review*, *Partisan Review*, *Prism International*, and *Translation*, as well as in most of the countries in Eastern and Western Europe. He spent a semester as visiting writer at the University of Iowa's International Writing Program and has given readings and lectures at many American universities. He moved to the United States in 1990 and lives in Boston, Massachusetts, with his son.

Index of Poets

■

Body type is in Bodoni
and titling is in Poster Bodoni.
Typeset by Villager Graphics.
Printed on acid-free Glatfelter
by Thomson-Shore, Inc.

Special thanks for:
Artworks by Georgi Alaikov.
Author photographs by Vanya Vassileva,
with the exception of Georgi Belev's photograph,
which was taken by Lisa Sapinkopf.